Ministry of Agriculture, Fisheries and Food
Department of Agriculture and Fisheries for Sco
Department of Agriculture for Northern Ireland

Energy allowances and feeding systems for ruminants

Reference Book 433

London   Her Majesty's Stationery Office

© Crown copyright 1984
First published 1975
Second edition 1984

ISBN 011 242642 5

Foreword

The decision to adopt a metabolisable energy (ME) system in place of the starch equivalent (SE), a net energy system, as the official advisory method for allocating energy allowances for ruminants, was taken at a joint conference on 'Nutrient Standards for Ruminants' held in London on 12 April 1972. This conference was held to consider reports of three working parties set up following an earlier conference at which the teaching and advisory implications of the ARC Review, 'Nutrient Requirements of Farm Livestock No 2—Ruminants' were discussed. Each working party has been asked to deal with the advisory implications of the ARC recommendations, one of which was to adopt an ME system on the principles suggested in the ARC report. The Energy Requirements Working Party undertook the task of evaluating the proposed ME system and of comparing it with the SE system in its ability to predict animal performance more acurately. The conclusion was reached that the new system was the superior and its adoption was recommended in a modified form better suited to advisory purposes. An outline of a modified version of the system was included in the report.

At the joint conference, the Chairman, the late Sir Ronald Baskett, expressed the view, which was agreed unanimously, that any proposed changes in nutritional standards or systems should be introduced on a United Kingdom basis. Consequently when, as a result of the joint conference, an ME System Working Party was set up with the object of seeking the most effective way of introducing a practical ME system in the United Kingdom, representatives from ADAS, the Department of Agriculture for Northern Ireland and the Scottish Agriculture Colleges were invited to serve on it. The members from ADAS were Messrs G. Alderman and D. E. Morgan (Chairman and Secretary respectively) who provided continuity from the previous working party, and Mr. A. Harvard who had taken a special interest in requirements for sheep and in tables of feed composition. From Northern Ireland, Professor J. R. Todd was able to bring experience in the use of the system for beef production. Dr. R. A. Edwards representing the Scottish College interests was an invaluable member because of his close association with the derivation by the Edinburgh School of Agriculture of a simple additive Variable Net Energy System from the original ARC proposals for growing and fattening animals. The Working Party decided that the principles of this net energy system should be adopted for use with the modified ME System. With Mr. Harvard, Dr. Edwards also prepared the present proposals for allowances for sheep. I should like to acknowledge the contributions of all members of the Working Party and to pay a special tribute to the enthusiasm and determination of its Chairman, Mr. G. Alderman.

The main function of this Working Party has been the preparation of this Technical Bulletin describing the derivation and use of the modified ME system in detail. This is the first bulletin to provide guidelines for the practical implementation of the modified ME system in the United Kingdom. Obviously research on all aspects of this topic continues. The present system is flexible and may be easily adjusted, when necessary, to include new data emerging from research. Further amendments to the bulletin will probably be needed during the next few years. The adoption of a policy of periodic review and revision will also meet another request, made at the joint conference, for a continued close liaison and exchange of ideas and information between advisers and research workers. Energy can be a major limiting factor in production from ruminants in the United Kingdom. It is hoped that those who use this bulletin in advisory work will find it helpful in overcoming many practical production problems related to energy requirements.

H. C. GOUGH
Chief Science Adviser
Agricultural Development
and Advisory Service

May 1975

Eight years have passed since the original publication of Technical Bulletin 33, now reprinted as Reference Book 433. During this time there have been several developments in our understanding of energy metabolism in ruminants, and in our ability to predict the ME values of foodstuffs. A comprehensive revision of the text would, however, be premature at this stage in view of the detailed consultations taking place on the ARC Working Party report on the 'Nutrient Requirements of Ruminant Livestock', 1980.

In this second edition, the main changes will be found on pages 72-74. They consist of revised regression equations to predict the ME values of forage and compound foods, together with a list of revised nutritive values of foods agreed by the Standing Committee on Tables of Feed Composition in 1983.

Diligent readers of this text may notice that in some of the calculations the figures used for the ME values of foods differ from the revised values given on page 74. The worked examples should therefore be regarded as illustrations of the methods to be used in ration formulation and performance prediction, rather than definitive solutions related to specific circumstances.

As the type for this edition has been reset, the opportunity has been taken to make minor corrections and modifications throughout the text.

G. ALDERMAN
Senior Nutrition Chemist
Agricultural Development
and Advisory Service

August 1983

Preface

This bulletin is intended to be used primarily by agricultural advisers and teachers in the field of animal production. It is the first in a series of publications which will be required for the practical implementation of energy systems for ruminants based on metabolisable energy. The arguments for this change and the derivation of the simplified metabolisable energy systems have already been discussed in the Proceedings of the Seventh Nutrition Conference for Feed Manufacturers (Nottingham University, 1973). The current text is therefore, in the main, devoid of scientific references to support statements made.

The basic principles used are essentially those outlined in Section 6 of the Agricultural Research Council's Technical Review No 2 *Ruminants,* 1965. Also included are variable net energy systems for cattle and sheep which are adaptations of the system published by Harkins, Edwards and McDonald in 1974, based on earlier work by MacHardy. This approach offers considerable advantages in ration formulation for growing cattle and sheep.

As a means of expressing the usually simple relationships from which the systems are assembled, simple linear equations are given, but all the basic calculations can be performed by using the tables in the text. The equations have either been derived from basic data or are a good fit to the data, and are intended for use where greater accuracy is desired or for use in mathematical modelling. Because of the modular nature of the systems, modification or extension of the individual relationships should be easy to incorporate as new research findings become available.

Since agreement was reached in 1972 that these systems should be put into use by the autumn of 1976, when agriculture is due to assume its metrication programme, metric (S.I.) units have been used throughout. Food analyses are given as g/kg dry matter in the text and in the tables of food composition. The latter have been calculated from details of digestible nutrients of food, listed in ADAS Advisory Paper No 11 *Nutrient Allowances and Composition of Feeding Stuffs for Ruminants,* by the use of coefficients suggested by the Oskar Kellner Institute workers at Rostock, GDR.

The authors are indebted to Mrs J. F. B. Altman, Rothamsted Experimental Station, for the computation of metabolisable energy values of foods, metrication and verification of these tables.

                                          GA   AH   JRT
                                        RAE   DEM

Contents

Preface

Section I—Principles

page
- 9   Food energy
- 11   Measurement of Metabolisable Energy
- 12   Metabolisable Energy of the ration
- 12   Metabolisable Energy concentration of rations

- 13   Metabolisable Energy requirements
- 13   Maintenance
- 14   Liveweight gain
- 15   Milk production
- 15   Mobilisation of body reserves
- 16   Pregnancy

- 17   A Net Energy system for growing animals
- 17   Net Energy requirements
- 17   Net Energy values of foods
- 20   Animal Production Level

- 20   Safety margins

Section II—Dairy cows

- 21   Calculation of Metabolisable Energy allowances
- 21   Maintenance   (Table 1a)
- 21   Milk production   (Tables 2,3)
- 23   Liveweight change
- 24   Daily ME allowances   (Table 4)
- 24   Pregnancy   (Table 5)

- 25   Appetite limits for dairy cows   (Table 6)

- 26   Checking a ration

- 27   Ration formulation
- 28   Rapid method   (Table 7)
- 29   Linear programming

page

30	Feeding the dairy cow
30	Significance of liveweight changes
30	Ration formulation for stages of lactation
32	Feeding according to yield
32	Energy requirements of grazing cows
32	Summary

Section III—Growing and fattening cattle

33	Prediction of performance
33	Ration calculations
33	Maintenance allowances (Table 1b)
34	Predicted liveweight gain (Tables 8,9)
37	Calculation of Metabolisable Energy allowances (Table 10)
39	Ration formulation
40	Rapid method (Table 11)
42	Linear programming
42	Net Energy system for ration formulation
43	Animal Production Level (Table 12)
44	Net Energy for maintenance and production
45	Net Energy values of foods (Table 13)
45	Net Energy allowances (Table 14)
45	Ration formulation
48	Replacement values of foods
48	Linear programming
49	Summary

Section IV—Sheep

51	Pregnant and lactating ewes
51	Maintenance allowances
51	Pregnancy allowances (Table 15)
53	Ration formulation
53	Lactation allowances (Tables 16,17,18)
54	Ration formulation
56	Growing and fattening sheep: performance prediction
56	Maintenance allowances (Table 19)
57	Prediction of liveweight gain (Tables 20,21)
60	Calculation of Metabolisable Energy allowances (Table 22)
60	Growing and fattening sheep: A Net Energy System
62	Net Energy allowances (Table 23)
62	Animal Production Level (Table 24)
64	Net Energy values of foods (Table 25)
65	Ration formulation
66	Replacement values of foods
66	Summary

Section V—Metabolisable Energies of foods

- 68 Energy values of foods
- 68 Digestibility measurements on foods
- 70 Metabolisable Energy values of foods
- 71   Prediction of the ME of forages
- 73   Estimation of the ME of compound foods
- 74 Revised nutritive values of foods
- 75 Tables of food composition

Terminology and symbols used

APL	Animal Production Level
BF	Butter Fat content (g/kg)
DM	Dry Matter content (g/kg)
DMI	Dry Matter Intake (kg/day)
EV_c	Energy Value of Concepta (MJ/kg)
EV_g	Energy Value of Gain (MJ/kg)
EV_l	Energy Value of Milk (MJ/kg)
E_g	Net Energy required for Body Gain (MJ/day)
E_l	Net Energy required for Milk Production (MJ/day)
E_m	Net Energy required for Maintenance (MJ/day)
E_p	Net Energy required for Production (MJ/day)
FM	Fasting Metabolism (MJ/day)
k_g	Efficiency of utilisation of ME for Body Gain
k_l	Efficiency of utilisation of ME for Milk Production
k_m	Efficiency of utilisation of ME for Maintenance
k_p	Efficiency of utilisation of ME for Production
k_{mp}	Efficiency of utilisation of ME for Maintenance and Production
LWG	Liveweight Gain (kg/day) or (g/day)
ME	Metabolisable Energy
MEF	ME of Food (MJ/kgDM)
MER	ME of Ration (MJ)
MEP	ME available for Production (MJ/day)
M_g	ME required for Body Gain (MJ/day)
M_l	ME required for Milk Production (MJ/day)
M_m	ME required for Maintenance (MJ/day)
M_p	ME required for Production (MJ/day)
M/D	ME concentration in Dry Matter (MJ/kgDM)
NE_g	Net Energy of a food or ration for Body Gain (MJ/kgDM)
NE_l	Net Energy of a food or ration for Maintenance and Lactation (MJ/kgDM)
NE_m	Net Energy of a food or ration for Maintenance (MJ/kgDM)
NE_p	Net Energy of a food or ration for Production (MJ/kgDM)

NE$_{mp}$ Net Energy of a food or ration for Maintenance and Production (MJ/kgDM)

SNF   Solids-Not-Fat content of milk (g/kg)
W   Liveweight (kg)
Y   Milk Yield (kg/day)

Section I—Principles

Food energy

At the present time the basic unit of energy used in nutrition is the thermochemical calorie (cal) based on the calorific value of benzoic acid as the reference standard. Usually the kilocalorie (kcal), equivalent to 1000 cal, or the megacalorie (Mcal), equivalent to 1,000,000 cal, are used in practice because the calorie is inconveniently small. The Royal Society has recommended that the calorie shall be replaced by the SI unit for energy, the joule (J). The joule-equivalent of the thermochemical calorie is 4.184J. By analogy with current practice the units employed will be the kilojoule (kJ) or the megajoule (MJ).

When a food is burned completely in a bomb calorimeter, energy is released and can be measured as heat. This is termed the 'heat of combustion', or more commonly the 'gross energy' of the food, and represents its total content of energy. Instead of gross energy, the recommended term 'energy value' (EV) is used in this bulletin. The energy value of an individual food is the sum of the energy values of its constituents. Carbohydrate, the dominant fraction of most foods, has an energy value of about 17.5 MJ/kg of dry matter. Fats contain about two and a half times, and protein about one and a half times as much energy as carbohydrates while ash has no energy. As the protein and/or fat content of a food increases so does its energy value. In contrast, foods of high ash content have low energy values. Since carbohydrate is the dominant fraction in most foods, energy values are normally about 18 MJ/kg of dry matter.

Not all the energy value of a food is available to the animal. Part of it, that which is not digested, is voided in the faeces and its energy lost to the animal. The difference between the energy value of the food and that of the associated faeces is the 'digestible energy' (DE) of the food. This concept assumes that all the food energy which does not appear in the faeces is digested and absorbed by the animal and that all faecal energy originates in the food. This is not strictly correct and the figure should be referred to as the 'apparently digestible energy', as distinct from the 'truly digestible energy' which is a rarely used concept. The digestibility of energy varies within wide limits for different foods. Thus in barley straw it is about 0.45 while in cereals such as barley it is about 0.85.

A further loss of energy from the alimentary canal occurs in the form of combustible gases, made up almost entirely of methane. This loss is particularly important in ruminant animals in which it amounts to about 0.08 of the energy value of the food at the maintenance level of intake but falls to about 0.06 as the level of intake rises. Energy is also lost from the body in urine which contains organic waste products of no further direct use to the animal. The difference between the apparently digestible energy of the food and the sum of the methane and urinary energy losses is termed the 'metabolisable energy' (ME). It represents that portion of the food energy which can be utilised by the animal. On average about 0.81 of the digestible energy is metabolisable.

Animals produce heat continuously and lose it to their surroundings, even when fasting. If a fasted animal consumes food, its heat production increases, mainly due to the inefficiency with which absorbed nutrients are used by the body. Energy is also used in the mastication of the food and its propulsion through the alimentary canal and is dissipated as heat. In ruminant animals a further heat loss takes place through the activities of the micro-organisms of the gut. This may amount to 0.05 to 0.10 of the energy value of the food. The increase in heat production, resulting from the consumption and utilisation of food, is termed the 'heat increment' (HI) and since the heat is of no use to the animal, except in a particularly cold environment, it is regarded as an inevitable loss from the energy of the food. Deduction of the heat increment from the metabolisable energy gives the 'net energy' of the food, which represents that part of the food energy which is used by the animal for maintenance and production. The fate of food energy within the animal is illustrated in Figure 1.

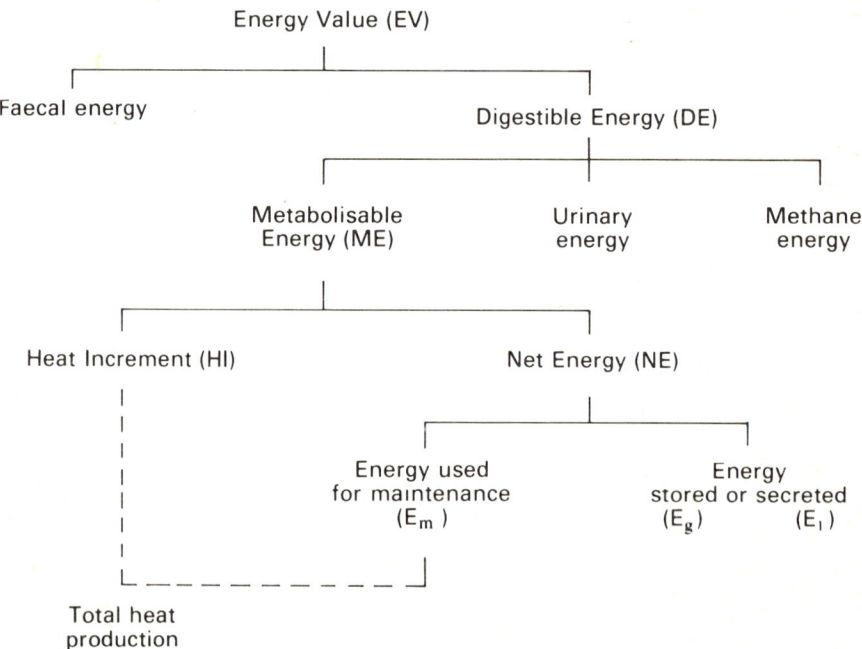

Fig 1 Partitioning of food energy within the animal

An example of an actual energy balance is given in Table A.

Table A—Partitioning of the energy of grass within the animal

Dry matter intake		= 1.829	kg
Energy intake		= 35.0	MJ
Faecal energy		= 13.5	MJ
Urinary energy		= 1.2	MJ
Methane energy		= 2.4	MJ
Heat increment		= 7.0	MJ
Digestible energy	$= \dfrac{35.0 - 13.5}{1.829}$	= 11.8	MJ/kg
Metabolisable energy	$= \dfrac{35.0 - (13.5 + 1.2 + 2.4)}{1.829}$	= 9.8	MJ/kg
Net energy	$= \dfrac{35.0 - (13.5 + 1.2 + 2.4 + 7.0)}{1.829}$	= 6.0	MJ/kg

Wainman FW, Smith JB & Blaxter KL
Proc. Nut. Soc. (1971) 30, 23A

Use of the Metabolisable Energy concept in the feeding of animals

A rationing system based on metabolisable energy involves a knowledge of the energy requirements of the animal, and the ability of the food to satisfy those requirements, in terms of metabolisable energy.

Measurement of Metabolisable Energy

The energy supplied by foods (and the animal's requirements for energy) are measured in large respiration chambers or calorimeters. Measurements are made of the animal's heat production whilst intake of food energy and energy losses in faeces, urine and methane are also recorded. Energy stored as fat and/or protein can also be calculated.

If a respiration chamber is not available, but faecal and urine losses are known from metabolism trials, the metabolisable energy of a food (MEF) can be calculated since the methane losses are assumed to be 0.08 of the energy value of the food.

If only digestibility data are available use may be made of the relationship:
$$ME = 0.81\ DE \qquad (1)$$

Alternatively factors may be used to convert the digestible nutrients of a food to ME values and these summed to give the value for the food. The factors used in this bulletin are those proposed by workers at the Oskar Kellner Institute at Rostock, GDR:

Metabolisable Energy (MJ/kg) =
$$0.0152\ DCP + 0.0342\ DEE + 0.0128\ DCF + 0.0159\ DNFE \qquad (2)$$

Where   DCP = Digestible crude protein g/kg
             DEE = Digestible ether extract g/kg

DCF = Digestible crude fibre g/kg
DNFE = Digestible nitrogen-free extractives g/kg

Example 1

	g/kg	Factor	ME(MJ)
DCP	90	0.0152	1.37
DEE	7	0.0342	0.24
DCF	221	0.0128	2.83
DNFE	354	0.0159	5.63
			10.07

Such approaches are conveniently used for concentrate foods since a chemical analysis can give the composition, and digestibility coefficients (as given in the tables of food composition) may be assumed for a given food with reasonable accuracy. With roughage foods this is not so because of the variability in their composition and the digestibilities of their constituents. With such foods it is usual to determine the level of a given constituent or constituents which may be related to the metabolisable energy in prediction equations. An example of this approach is the equation for predicting the metabolisable energy of hay from its content of modified acid detergent fibre:

$$ME (MJ/kgDM) = 16.37 - 0.0205\ MADF \qquad (3)$$

MADF = Modified acid detergent fibre in dry matter (g/kgDM)

Details are given in Section V of recommended equations for various classes of foods.

The ME values of foods (designated MEF) are usually stated in terms of the ME concentration in the dry matter, MJ/kgDM.

Metabolisable Energy of the ration

The metabolisable energy of the ration (MER) is calculated by summing the contributions of the individual foods making up the diet, and is expressed in terms of MJ of ME.

Metabolisable Energy concentration of rations

The energy concentration (M/D) of a ration is the ME per kilogram of ration dry matter and is expressed as MJ/kg DM. Its calculation is a simple matter and is necessary for ration calculations for beef cattle and lambs.

Example 2—Calculation of M/D of a ration

A ration consists of:

	DMI (kg)	ME (MJ)
6 kg hay, (850 g/kg DM, 8 MJ/kg DM)	5.1	40.8
3 kg cereal, (830 g/kg DM, 13 MJ/kg DM)	2.5	32.4
	7.6	73.2

$$\text{Metabolisable Energy concentration} = \frac{\text{Total ME of ration, (MER)}}{\text{Total dry matter intake, (DMI)}}$$

$$\text{Thus M/D} = \frac{\text{MER}}{\text{DMI}} = \frac{73.2}{7.6} = 9.6\ \text{MJ/kg DM}$$

Metabolisable Energy requirements

To formulate a requirement in terms of metabolisable energy the amount of net energy (NE) required must be known together with the efficiency (k) with which dietary metabolisable energy (ME) is used to satisfy that requirement. Then

$$k\ ME = NE$$
$$\text{or} \quad \frac{NE}{k} = ME$$

Animals require energy for the maintenance of essential life processes such as respiration and the circulation of blood. In addition, energy is required to provide the energy stored in various body tissues during growth and for products such as milk, and to actuate the synthetic processes involved in their production.

Maintenance

Energy used for maintenance is used for work and is dissipated as heat which is lost from the body. In the fasted animal this is derived from oxidation of body tissues and is termed the Fasting Metabolism (FM), representing the minimal requirement for energy to maintain the animal. It may be measured in a calorimeter, but in practice is usually estimated by means of equations (based on calorimetric measurements) such as

$$FM(MJ/day) = 5.67 + 0.061\ W \tag{4}$$
$$\text{where } W = \text{liveweight in kg}$$

which is a general one for growing cattle. Depending on the conditions under which animals are kept, an extra allowance of energy may be added to the fasting metabolism to allow for physical activity inseparable from the existence of the animal. This is referred to as an 'activity increment' and is usually about 0.1 of the fasting metabolism.

The efficiency with which ME is used for maintenance (k_m) is related to the energy concentration (M/D) of the ration and may be calculated as follows:

$$k_m = 0.55 + 0.016\ M/D \tag{5}$$
$$\text{where } M/D = \text{MJ per kg of dry matter.}$$

Over a range of dietary ME concentrations from 8 to 14 MJ/kgDM, k_m varies from 0.68 to 0.77. In practice such dietary extremes are found only infrequently, and adoption of a single value of 0.72 for k_m involves little error.

Example 3
Calculation of the ME requirement for maintenance, (M_m) of a 400 kg steer.
Fasting Metabolism, FM = 5.67 + (0.061 × 400) = 30.1 MJ/day
k_m = 0.72
ME requirement, $M_m = \dfrac{30.1}{0.72}$ = 42 MJ/day

Liveweight gain
The net energy requirement for gain (E_g) is the energy content of that gain and is the product of the weight of the gain (LWG) and its energy value (EV_g). For cattle, the energy value of gain is related to the liveweight in kg (W), and the energy stored in MJ (E_g), and may be calculated using the following equation:

$$EV_g \text{ (MJ/kg)} = 6.28 + 0.3\, E_g + 0.0188\, W \qquad (6)$$

Since $E_g = \text{LWG} \times EV_g$

Then $E_g = \dfrac{\text{LWG}\,(6.28 + 0.0188\, W)}{(1 - 0.3\, \text{LWG})}$ MJ (7)

The efficiency of utilisation of ME for body gain (k_g) varies considerably for different types of food. These variations as they affect the total ration can be related to the energy concentration of the ration and k_g may be calculated as follows:

$$k_g = 0.0435\, M/D \qquad (8)$$

Thus k_g can vary from about 0.30 to 0.60 as M/D varies from 7 to 14 MJ/kgDM

Example 4
Calculation of the ME requirement of a 400 kg steer gaining at 0.75 kg/day and fed a ration of M/D 10 MJ/kgDM.

ME required for maintenance, M_m = 42 MJ/day   (from Example 3)
$E_g = \dfrac{0.75\,[6.28 + (0.0188 \times 400)]}{[1 - (0.3 \times 0.75)]}$
= 13.4 MJ
k_g = 0.0435 × 10
= 0.435

ME required for body gain, $M_g = \dfrac{13.4}{0.435} = 30.8$ MJ

Total daily requirement for ME   = 42 + 30.8 = 73 MJ

Example 5
Prediction of liveweight gain of a 400 kg steer receiving 8.1 kg of a ration with a dry matter content of 900 g/kg with an M/D of 10 MJ/kgDM.

Total ME intake per day   = $8.1 \times \dfrac{900}{1000} \times 10 = 72.9$ MJ
ME required for maintenance, M_m = 42 MJ/day   (from Example 3)
ME available for production,   MEP = 72.9 − 42 = 30.9 MJ/day
k_g = 0.0435 × 10
= 0.435
E_g = 30.9 × 0.435 = 13.4 MJ/day
Energy value of gain EV_g = 6.28 + 0.3 E_g + 0.0188 W   (6)
= 6.28 + (0.3 × 13.4) + (0.0188 × 400)
= 17.8 MJ/kg

Predicted liveweight gain, LWG = $\dfrac{E_g}{EV_g} = \dfrac{13.4}{17.8} = 0.75$ kg/day

To obtain LWG directly, use
$$\text{LWG} = \frac{E_g}{(6.28 + 0.3\,E_g + 0.0188\,W)} \qquad (9)$$

Milk production

The minimal requirement for energy for milk production (E_l) is the product of the weight of milk (Y) in kg and its energy value (EV_l). For cow's milk the energy value is calculated as follows:

EV_l (MJ/kg) = 0.0386 BF + 0.0205 SNF − 0.236 (10)

where BF = butter fat content (g/kg)
SNF = solids-not-fat content (g/kg)

The composition of milk is not always known and it may be necessary to adopt averages for different breeds. Alternatively, milk production may be related to a base of solids-corrected milk (SCM) with a butterfat of 40 g/kg and a solids-not-fat content of 89 g/kg, or to an average milk having a butterfat of 36 g/kg and a solids-not-fat content of 86 g/kg.

The efficiency of utilisation of ME for milk production (k_l) is related to the ME concentration of the diet. Over the range of concentrations normally encountered with dairy cow diets the variation in k_l is not great and little error is incurred by the adoption of a single value of 0.62. The ME requirement for the production of 1 kg of milk is given by

$$\frac{EV_l}{0.62} \text{ or } 1.61\,EV_l$$

and the ME required (M_l) for the production of Y kg of milk is given by

$$M_l\,(MJ) = 1.61\,EV_l \times Y \qquad (11)$$

Mobilisation of body reserves

Energy other than that of the food may become available for milk production owing to the mobilisation of the body reserves of the lactating animal. The energy value of body tissue thus mobilised is about 20 MJ/kg. This can be used for milk production with an efficiency of 0.82. Hence 1 kg body weight loss would produce 20 × 0.82 = 16.4 MJ as milk, equivalent to 5.2 kg solids corrected milk.

ME is used for body gain in the *lactating* dairy cow with the same efficiency, 0.62, as for lactation. A gain in weight of 1 kg thus increases the animal's requirement for ME by

$$\frac{20}{0.62} = 32.3\text{ MJ}$$

This high efficiency for gain, (k_g) of 0.62, only applies whilst cows are lactating. Dry cows gain weight less efficiently and the same values of k_g as for growing cattle are suggested, as in Section III of this book and Example 4 of this section.

Pregnancy

The pregnant animal requires energy to maintain itself and the developing foetus. In addition, energy is stored in the foetus and associated membranes and in accrued uterine tissues, and is required for the syntheses involved in their production. The energy stored daily in the uterus and the uterine contents increases exponentially throughout pregnancy and is of considerable significance in the final stages. For cattle the daily energy deposition (E_c) may be estimated by equations such as the following:

Uterine Deposition of Energy, $E_c = 0.03\ e^{0.0174t}$ (MJ/day) (12)

where t = the number of days after conception

and e = 2.718, the base of the natural logarithm.

Heat production in pregnant animals is greater than expected for non-pregnant animals of similar weights. The increased heat production is termed the 'Heat Increment of Gestation' (HIG) and may be calculated for cattle as follows:

Heat Increment of Gestation, $HIG = 0.904\ e^{0.01t}$ (MJ/day) (13)

where t = the number of days after conception

and e = 2.718.

About half the heat increment of gestation arises from the synthetic processes producing the foetus and associated structures. The remainder arises from the energy used for foetal maintenance and the increase in maternal fasting metabolism occuring in pregnancy.

Thus the ME requirement for the growth of the foetus and associated structures will be the sum of the energy stored, (E_c) plus half the heat increment of gestation, i.e., $E_c + \dfrac{HIG}{2}$ MJ/day.

The energy for foetal and increased maternal maintenance may be assumed to be provided from dietary ME with the usual efficiency of 0.72 and the ME requirement is then

$$\dfrac{HIG}{2 \times 0.72}$$

The extra ME requirement for pregnancy will therefore be

$$E_c + \dfrac{HIG}{2} + \dfrac{HIG}{2 \times 0.72}\ MJ/day$$

which becomes

ME requirement = $E_c + 1.19\ HIG$ (14)

Values for E_c and HIG can be obtained from equations (12) and (13), and values for ($E_c \times 1.19\ HIG$) are given by the equation

$E_c + 1.19\ HIG = 1.08\ e^{0.0106t}$ MJ/day (15)

where t = number of days after conception

and e = 2.718

The total ME requirement of a pregnant cow will therefore be:

$M_m + 1.08\ e^{0.0106t}$ MJ/day (16)

Example 6
Calculation of the ME requirement of a 500 kg cow producing a 40 kg calf at birth, at 250 days after conception.
  ME required for normal maternal maintenance, M_m = 50.2 MJ/day
  Heat increment of gestation, HIG = $0.904\ e^{0.01 \times 250}$ = 11.0 MJ/day
  Energy stored in foetus E_c = $0.03\ e^{0.0174 \times 250}$ = 2.3 MJ/day
  ME requirement = $M_m + E_c + 1.19$ HIG
                 = 50.2 + 2.3 + (1.19 × 11.0) MJ/day
                 = 65.6 MJ/day

Use of a Net Energy system for growing animals

The metabolisable energy system provides a suitable method for predicting performance in growing animals but does not allow easy, convenient formulation of rations. To formulate a ration it is necessary to know the metabolisable energy requirements for growth and therefore the metabolisable energy concentration of the ration. Obviously this cannot be known until the ration is formulated. The problem can be overcome by using various procedures but a simpler method is to eliminate the dependence of requirement upon the metabolisable energy concentration of the ration. This can be achieved by using a net energy requirement. The net energy values of foods must then be known if rations are to be formulated.

Net Energy requirements
The net energy requirements for maintenance (E_m) and growth (E_g) have already been discussed and may be calculated as

$$E_m (MJ/day) = 5.67 + 0.061\ W \qquad (4)$$

$$E_g (MJ/day) = \frac{LWG\ (6.28 + 0.0188\ W)}{(1 - 0.3\ LWG)} \qquad (7)$$

In a general sense E_g may be replaced by E_p, the net energy required for production.

Net Energy values of foods
The net energy value of a diet for maintenance (NE_m) may be calculated as:
$$NE_m = M_m \times k_m$$
and for production
$$NE_p = M_p \times k_p$$
In a productive situation the net energy of a food is a combination of NE_m and NE_p i.e., NE_{mp}, the net energy for maintenance and production, which may be calculated as:
$$NE_{mp} = M_{mp} \times k_{mp} \qquad (17)$$

If we consider two diets of MEF 14 (1) and 10 (2) given at a single level of production we have a situation illustrated in Fig. 2.

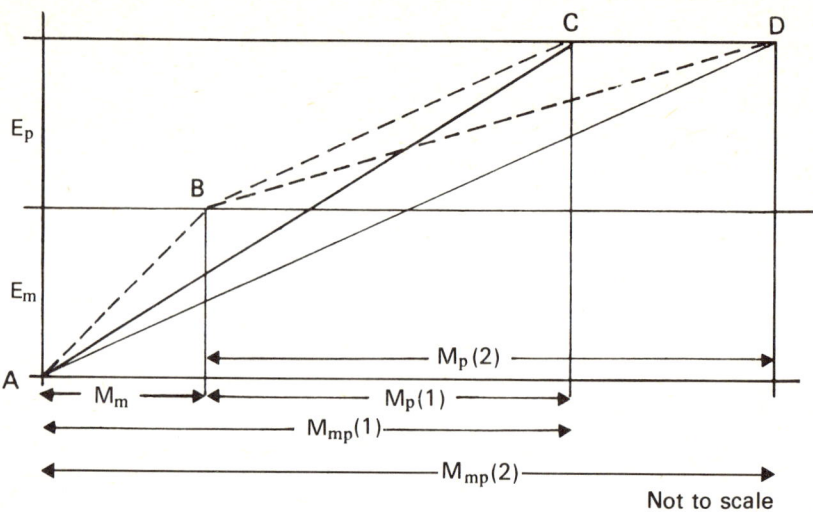

M_m is the same in both cases
$M_p(1)$ is the ME required for production at M/D 14 MJ/kgDM
$M_p(2)$ is the ME required for production at M/D 10 MJ/kgDM

Fig. 2 Net Energies of two diets at the same level of animal production

The efficiency of utilisation of dietary metabolisable energy for maintenance (k_m) for both diets is the slope of the line AB. The slope of line BC gives the efficiency of utilisation of dietary metabolisable energy for production (k_p) for a diet of M/D 14 while the slope of the line BD gives k_p for a diet of M/D 10. The efficiencies of utilisation for the combined functions of maintenance and growth (k_{mp}) are given by the slopes of AC and AD for the diets of M/D 14 and 10 respectively. This can be expressed as

$$k_{mp} = \frac{E_m + E_p}{M_{mp}} \qquad (18)$$

where E_m = net energy for maintenance as given in equation (4)

E_p = net energy for body gain given by equation (7)

and M_{mp} = the metabolisable energy required for maintenance and production.

On the other hand, if we consider the situation of a single diet with an M/D of say 10 given at two levels of production we have the situation illustrated in Fig. 3.

At a level of production one and a half times E_m, k_{mp} is given by the slope of the line AC and for a level of twice E_m by the slope of AD.

It is clear that k_{mp} varies with metabolisable energy concentration of the diet and with level of production, and it follows that the net energies of foods will be different for different productive situations and must be calculated afresh each time.

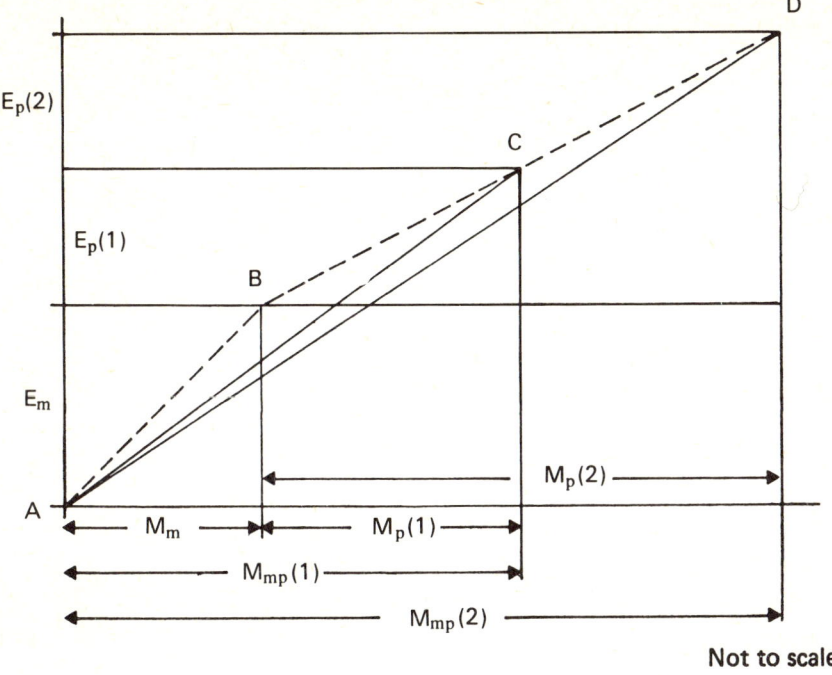

Fig 3 Net Energies of the same diet at two levels of animal production

Example 7
Formulation of a ration from hay (MEF 8.5 MJ/kg DM) and compound food (MEF 13 MJ/kg DM) for a 400 kg steer growing at 0.75 kg/day.

$$E_m = 30.1 \text{ MJ} \quad (4)$$

$$E_p = 13.4 \text{ MJ} \quad (7)$$

If only hay were fed, the theoretical ME requirement for a ration of M/D 8.5 MJ/kg DM would be 78 MJ, i.e.,

$$M_{mp} \text{ for hay} = 78 \text{ MJ}$$

$$\text{hence } k_{mp} \text{ for hay} = \frac{30.1 + 13.4}{78} = 0.558$$

$$\text{and } NE_{mp} \text{ for hay} = 8.5 \times 0.558 = 4.74 \text{ MJ/kg DM}$$

Similarly if only a compound food were fed, the theoretical ME requirement would be

$$M_{mp} \text{ for compound food} = 65.5 \text{ MJ}$$

$$k_{mp} \text{ for compound food} = \frac{30.1 + 13.4}{65.5} = 0.664$$

$$NE_{mp} \text{ for compound food} = 13.0 \times 0.66 = 8.63 \text{ MJ/kg DM}$$

$$\text{Total net energy required } (E_{mp}) = 30.1 + 13.4 = 43.5 \text{ MJ/day}$$

This may be provided by hay alone (a), compound food alone (b), or a combination (c). The amounts needed are:

(a) Hay required $= \dfrac{43.5}{4.74} = 9.2$ kg dry matter

(b) Compound food required $= \dfrac{43.5}{8.63} = 5.0$ kg dry matter

(c) Hay required to feed with 3 kg compound food dry matter

$$= \dfrac{43.5 - (3.0 \times 8.63)}{4.74} = 3.7 \text{ kg dry matter}$$

Such calculations are laborious and time consuming and are only acceptable when sophisticated computer facilities are available. In the absence of these facilities considerable improvement can be achieved by making use of the fact that NE_{mp} is constant for foods or rations of a particular M/D at a specified level of production. The effect of the latter can be quantified by relating it to the animal production level (APL).

Animal Production Level
This term was first suggested by MacHardy in 1965, who defined it as

$$\text{Animal Production Level, APL} = \dfrac{E_m + E_p}{E_m} \quad \text{or} \quad 1 + \dfrac{E_p}{E_m} \qquad (19)$$

This approach has been called 'scaling by fasting metabolism' and resembles the use of 'x times maintenance' as a method of describing plane of nutrition irrespective of body size. Animals at maintenance have an APL value of 1.0 since by definition $E_p = 0$ at maintenance.

Tables of NE_{mp} values for foods of different metabolisable energy concentrations at different APL values may be constructed. The APL for a given situation may then be calculated and used, along with the M/D values of the foods available, to enter the tables of NE_{mp} values. These may then be used as shown in Example 7. The use of the tables is discussed in detail in Section III of this book.

Safety margins

The Ministry of Agriculture, Fisheries and Food Energy Working Party which reported in 1972 recommended that ME requirements should be increased by a factor of 0.05 to make them ME 'allowances'. No firm statistical basis was given for this safety margin, but considerations of the known variability of fasting metabolism measurements and the variations in the ME values of foods were felt to justify such a recommendation. In the sections on dairy cattle and sheep which follow, a safety margin has been included in all the tables. This should be borne in mind when comparing these sections with this introductory section where no safety margins are included in the examples and calculations.

Section II—Use of the Metabolisable Energy system for dairy cows

Calculation of Metabolisable Energy allowances

As discussed in Section I, the use of the ME system for dairy cattle involves the separate calculation of the maintenance and production allowances which are then summed to give a total ME allowance. This figure may have to be modified in the light of weight changes taking place in the animal.

Metabolisable Energy allowances for maintenance
The net energy requirement for maintenance is the fasting metabolism plus any activity allowance deemed necessary. Fasting metabolism for the cow may be taken as 0.36 MJ/kg $W^{0.73}$, which with a 0.1 activity increment gives a net energy requirement (E_m) of 0.396 MJ/kg $W^{0.73}$.

The efficiency of utilisation of ME for maintenance (k_m) is assumed to be constant at 0.72, and the ME requirement for maintenance M_m can be calculated from

$$M_m = \frac{E_m}{k_m} = \frac{0.396 \text{ MJ/kg } W^{0.73}}{0.72}$$
$$= 0.55 \text{ MJ/kg } W^{0.73}$$

Addition of a safety margin of 0.05 gives a total allowance of 0.58 MJ/kg $W^{0.73}$. There is little loss of precision if a simple linear equation is used, so that ME allowances for maintenance (M_m) are given by

$$M_m = 8.3 + 0.091 W \qquad (20)$$

where M_m = maintenance allowance in MJ/day
and W = liveweight in kg

The maintenance allowances M_m, for cows of various liveweights are shown in Table 1a (see page 22).

Metabolisable Energy allowances for milk production
The net energy requirement for milk production (E_l) is the energy of the milk secreted. This depends upon the milk yield (Y) and the energy value of the milk (EV_l). The energy value of the milk secreted is calculated from the equation

$$EV_l = 0.0386 \text{ BF} + 0.0205 \text{ SNF} - 0.236 \qquad (10)$$

where EV_l is the energy value of the milk secreted in MJ/kg
and BF and SNF are in g/kg of milk

The efficiency of utilisation of ME for milk production (k_l) is assumed to be constant at 0.62. The ME requirement for milk production, M_l) is given by $\frac{EV_l}{0.62}$, which with the inclusion of a 0.05 safety margin becomes

$$M_l = 1.694\ EV_l\ \text{MJ/kg milk} \qquad (21)$$

The ME allowances for the production of 1 kg of milk from different breeds of cow are tabulated in Table 2.

Table 1a—Daily maintenance allowance of ME for dairy cows

Body weight (kg)	MJ/head
100	17
150	22
200	27
250	31
300	36
350	40
400	45
450	49
500	54
550	59
600	63

(including safety margin)
Based on $M_m = 8.3 + 0.091\ W$

Table 2—ME allowances for 1 kg milk

Type of milk	BF (g/kg)	SNF (g/kg)	Energy value EV_l, (MJ/kg)	ME allowance M_l, (MJ/kg)
Channel Island	48	91	3.482	5.90
Shorthorn	36	87	2.937	4.98
Ayrshire	37	88	2.996	5.08
Friesian	36	86	2.917	4.94
Average	38	87	3.014	5.10
Solids corrected	40	89	3.133	5.31

(including safety margin)
Based on $M_l = 1.694\ EV_l$

If the butter fat (BF) and solids-not-fat (SNF) values for the milk are known, the ME allowance for 1 kg of milk of any quality can be found in Table 3. (Note: BF and SNF values are g/kg = 10 × BF% or SNF%)

Example 8
Calculation of the ME allowance for a Friesian cow weighing 590 kg giving 20 kg milk at 36 g/kg BF and 86 g/kg SNF.

The total allowance for maintenance M_m = 63 MJ (Table 1)
Milk of 36 g/kg BF and 86 g/kg SNF requires 4.94 MJ/kg of milk (Table 3)
Hence a milk yield of 20 kg requires 20 × 4.94 = 99 MJ ME
So M_l required is 99 MJ
Total ME allowance = 62 + 99 = 161 MJ/day (Table 4)

Table 3—Metabolisable Energy allowance (MJ) to produce 1 kg milk of varying composition

SNF content (g/kg)	Fat content of milk (g/kg)										
	30	32	34	36	38	40	42	44	46	48	50	52
84	4.48	4.61	4.74	4.87	5.00	5.13	5.26	5.39	5.52	5.65	5.79	5.92
85	4.51	4.64	4.77	4.90	5.04	5.17	5.30	5.43	5.56	5.69	5.82	5.95
86	4.55	4.68	4.81	4.94	5.07	5.20	5.33	5.46	5.59	5.72	5.85	5.99
87	4.58	4.71	4.84	4.98	5.10	5.24	5.37	5.50	5.63	5.76	5.89	6.02
88	4.62	4.75	4.88	5.01	5.14	5.27	5.40	5.53	5.66	5.79	5.92	6.05
89	4.65	4.78	4.91	5.04	5.17	5.31	5.44	5.57	5.70	5.83	5.96	6.09
90	4.69	4.82	4.95	5.08	5.21	5.34	5.47	5.60	5.73	5.86	5.99	6.12
91	4.72	4.85	4.98	5.11	5.24	5.37	5.51	5.64	5.77	5.90	6.03	6.16
92	4.76	4.89	5.02	5.15	5.28	5.41	5.54	5.67	5.80	5.93	6.06	6.19
93	4.79	4.92	5.05	5.18	5.31	5.44	5.57	5.71	5.84	5.97	6.10	6.23
94	4.82	4.96	5.09	5.22	5.35	5.48	5.61	5.74	5.87	6.00	6.13	6.26
95	4.86	4.99	5.12	5.25	5.38	5.51	5.64	5.77	5.91	6.04	6.17	6.30

(Including safety margin)

⌐ ⌐ Milk of average composition   ☐ Solids corrected milk (SCM)

Significance of liveweight change in the calculation of ME allowance
If a cow's ration is deficient in energy, the deficit is made up from the body reserves of the cow with a resultant loss in weight. In Section I an outline was given of the quantitative aspects of this important question.

Briefly, body tissue has an energy value of 20 MJ/kg and can be used with an efficiency of 0.82 for milk production. Thus each kg of tissue mobilised will allow the secretion of 20 × 0.82 = 16.4 MJ as milk. This is equivalent to a dietary ME of

$$\frac{16.4 \times 1.05}{0.62} = 28 \text{ MJ (including safety margin)}$$

To summarise: **1kg liveweight loss equals 28 MJ of dietary ME.**

Example 8 continued
The Friesian cow is known to be losing 0.5 kg per day whilst producing the 20 kg milk.

Total ME allowance (no weight change) = 161 MJ/day
ME available from liveweight loss (M_g) = 28 × 0.5 = 14 MJ/day
So that total ME allowance = 161 — 14
= 147 MJ/day   (Table 4)

Body tissue is laid down with a higher efficiency (k_g) in the lactating compared with the non-lactating animal, and has a similar value to k_l of 0.62. The dietary ME allowance for gain is therefore

$$M_g = \frac{20}{0.62} \times 1.05 = 34 \text{ MJ/kg gain (including safety margin)}$$

so **ME allowance for 1 kg liveweight gain is 34 MJ dietary ME**

Allowances for body gain have to be added to those for maintenance and milk production in the calculation of ME allowances for animals gaining weight.

Example 8 continued
If the cow in this example is gaining 0.5 kg/day instead of losing it,
total ME allowance (no weight change)   = 161 MJ/day
ME allowance for weight gain = 0.5 × 34 =   17 MJ/day
then total ME allowance   = 161 + 17   = 178 MJ/day   (Table 4)

Daily allowances of ME for dairy cows

Suggested daily allowances of ME for three common breeds of dairy cattle are given in Table 4. They include an adjustment for liveweight change, but it must be remembered that the data can only be used to predict milk yield or liveweight change if the other is known.

Table 4 can be used to check the energy requirement of a cow whose milk yield is known and to quantify the effect of any energy deficit or surplus. When formulating rations it is important to consider the stage of lactation and desired liveweight change, as well as expected milk yield. A typical liveweight change pattern for a lactation is given later in this section.

Metabolisable Energy allowances for pregnancy

Details are given in Section I of the basis for calculating the ME allowances for pregnancy. These can be calculated readily from the equation

ME for maintenance and pregnancy = $M_m + 1.13\ e^{0.0106t}$ MJ/day   (16)

where   t = number of days pregnant
and   e = 2.718, the base of natural logarithms.

The calculated ME allowances are less than 5 MJ/day above maintenance up to the fifth month of pregnancy, hence allowances are shown in Table 5 from the sixth month of pregnancy only.

Table 4—Daily ME allowances for three breeds of dairy cattle (MJ/head)

Breed	Liveweight change	Main-tenance	Milk yield kg/day					
			5	10	15	20	25	30	35
JERSEY									
400 kg	Losing 0.5 kg/day	—	61	91	121	152	183		
49 g/kg BF	No weight change	45	75	105	135	166	197		
95 g/kg SNF	Gaining 0.5 kg/day	—	92	122	152	183	214		
AYRSHIRE									
500 kg	Losing 0.5 kg/day	—	66	92	118	144	169	195	
38 g/kg BF	No weight change	54	80	106	132	158	183	209	
89 g/kg SNF	Gaining 0.5 kg/day	—	97	123	149	175	200	226	
FRIESIAN									
590 kg	Losing 0.5 kg/day	—	73	97	122	147	172	196	221
36 g/kg BF	No weight change	62	87	111	136	161	186	210	235
86 g/kg SNF	Gaining 0.5 kg/day	—	104	128	153	178	203	227	252

(including safety margin)

Table 5—Daily ME allowances for cattle during pregnancy (MJ/head)

Liveweight (kg)	Month of pregnancy			
	6	7	8	9
350	48	51	55	60
400	52	55	59	65
450	57	60	64	69
500	61	64	68	74
550	66	69	73	78
600	71	73	77	83
650	75	78	82	87
700	80	83	86	92

(including safety margin)

Based on $M_{mp} = M_m + 1.13e^{0.0106t}$

where t = number of days pregnant

Appetite limits for dairy cows

Sound ration formulation for dairy cattle requires that some estimate is made of their probable dry matter appetite under the conditions in which they are housed and fed. Appetite is influenced by body size and to some extent by milk yield and stage of lactation. There are a number of properties of foods which affect dry matter intake such as digestibility, processing and method of conservation of forage, as well as the nature of the feeding system and timing of feeds. It is difficult to quantify these factors satisfactorily, and estimates of intake have to rely largely on the experience and judgement of the feeder. The following equation has been found generally useful for mid and late lactation cows fed mixed diets:

$$DMI = 0.025\ W + 0.1\ Y \qquad (22)$$

where DMI = dry matter intake, kg/day

W = liveweight, kg

Y = milk yield, kg/day

In early lactation (the first 10 weeks) appetite is known to be reduced, probably by 2-3 kg/day below the values given by this equation. Estimates of probable dry matter intakes for cows of different weights and producing different quantities of milk are given in Table 6.

Table 6—Probable dry matter intake of cows in mid and late lactation (kg/day)

Liveweight, W (kg)	Milk yield, Y (kg/day)							
	5	10	15	20	25	30	35	40
350	9.3	9.8	10.3	10.8	11.3	11.8		
400	10.5	11.0	11.5	12.0	12.5	13.0		
450	11.8	12.3	12.8	13.3	13.8	14.3	14.8	
500	13.0	13.5	14.0	14.5	15.0	15.5	16.0	
550	14.3	14.8	15.3	15.8	16.3	16.8	17.3	17.8
600	15.5	16.0	16.5	17.0	17.5	18.0	18.5	19.0
650	16.8	17.3	17.8	18.3	18.8	19.3	19.8	20.3
700	18.0	18.5	19.0	19.5	20.0	20.5	21.0	21.5

Based on DMI (kg/day) = 0.025 W + 0.1 Y

Note: In the first 6 weeks of lactation, reduce these values by 2-3 kg DMI per day

Checking the adequacy of a given dairy cow ration

To do this the following data are needed:
(a) cow's liveweight, W (kg)
(b) cow's milk yield, Y (kg/day)
(c) cow's milk quality, BF and SNF, (g/kg)
(d) total ME supplied by the ration, MER (MJ/day)

and it is necessary to calculate:
(e) ME required for maintenance, M_m (MJ/day)
(f) ME available for production, MEP (MJ/day)
(g) ME required for known milk production, M_l (MJ)
(h) the difference if any between MEP and M_l

and to interpret this difference M_g in terms of liveweight change.

Example 9
A Friesian heifer in late lactation weighs 500 kg, has a milk yield of 10 kg, and is being fed a ration of

	DMI (kg)	ME (MJ)
3 kg hay, (850 g/kg DM and 8 MJ/kg DM)	2.55	20.4
30 kg maize silage, (250 g/kg DM and 10 MJ/kg DM)	7.50	75.0
3 kg compound food,(860 g/kg DM and 12.5 MJ/kg DM)	2.58	32.3
	12.63	127.7

Ration ME (MER) = 128 MJ
Probable dry matter intake, DMI = (0.025 × 500) + (0.1 × 10) kg
= 13.5 kg/day
hence the ration is feasible.

ME for maintenance, M_m	= 54 MJ	(Table 1)
ME for production, MEP	= 128 — 54 = 74 MJ	
ME for milk production, M_l	= 10 × 4.9 = 49 MJ	(Table 2)
Difference, M_g	= + 25 MJ	

1 kg liveweight gain requires 34 MJ per day
Therefore it is concluded that the ration is more than adequate for milk production, and that this heifer is gaining weight at a rate of

$$\frac{25}{34} = 0.74 \text{ kg/day}$$

Formulation of rations to support desired levels of milk production

The following information is required before proceeding:
(a) liveweight of the cow, W (kg)
(b) desired liveweight change, ± kg/day
(c) milk yield expected, Y (kg/day)
(d) milk quality, BF and SNF (g/kg)
(e) ME content of the available foods (MJ/kg DM)
(f) dry matter content of the foods (g/kg)
(g) dry matter appetite of the cow (kg/day)
and to calculate:
(h) ME allowance for maintenance, M_m (MJ/day)
(i) ME allowance for production, M_p (MJ/day)
(j) total ME allowance, $M_m + M_p$ (MJ/day)
(k) total DM and ME supplied by the foods making up the ration and to compare these with (j) and (g)

Example 10
An Ayrshire cow weighing 500 kg is expected to produce 25 kg milk per day with a liveweight loss of not more than 0.5 kg/day. BF is 38 g/kg, SNF is 89 g/kg and appetite expected to be 15 kg DM.

Foods available: grass silage, 200 g/kg DM, 9 MJ/kg DM
rolled barley, 850 g/kg DM, 13.7 MJ/kg DM
dairy compound, 860 g/kg DM, 12.5 MJ/kg DM

ME for maintenance M_m = 54 MJ (Table 1)
ME for production M_p = 25 × 5.17 = 129 MJ (Table 3)
Contribution from
liveweight loss, M_g = 0.5 × 28 = 14 MJ
Minimum ME required = $M_m + M_l + M_g$ = 54 + 129 − 14
= 169 MJ/day (Table 4)

Trial ration

		DMI (kg)	ME (MJ)
40 kg silage,	(200 g/kg DM, 9 MJ/kg DM)	8.0	72.0
4 kg barley,	(850) g/kg DM, 13.7 MJ/kg DM)	3.4	46.6
6 kg compound food,	(860 g/kg DM, 12.5 MJ/kg DM)	5.2	64.5
		16.6	183.1

This ration meets the full energy demand of the cow, 183 MJ (Table 4), and no liveweight loss would be likely. Since, however, the dry matter appetite was stated to be only 15 kg, the ration will not be fully consumed. If the silage intake is reduced by 8 kg/day the ration becomes

		DMI (kg)	ME (MJ)
32 kg silage,	(200 g/kg DM, 9 MJ/kg DM)	6.4	57.6
4 kg barley,	(850 g/kg DM, 13.7 MJ/kg DM)	3.4	46.6
6 kg compound food,	(860 g/kg DM, 12.5 MJ/kg DM)	5.2	64.5
		15.0	168.7

The total ME required is now close to the minimum of 169 MJ allowing for 0.5 kg liveweight loss per day, an acceptable, and probably unavoidable figure.

It must be remembered that prediction of dairy cattle performance from a knowledge of the dietary energy input is fraught with difficulties, because cows have two alternative forms of output, milk and liveweight gain (or loss). The partitioning of production energy between liveweight and milk is difficult to quantify. Several factors which influence it have been identified, e.g., early lactation feeding level, current stage of lactation, nature of the diet. If the dietary intake and milk yield of a cow are known, calculations will indicate whether that cow's energy requirements are being met adequately, as shown earlier in this section.

Rapid formulation of forage and compound food rations

In the case of two component systems i.e. forage and compound food only, the energy concentration of the ration (M/D) can be used as a method of calculating rations which meet both dry matter appetite limits and energy allowances.

By definition, ration energy concentration, $M/D = \dfrac{\text{ME allowance (MJ)}}{\text{DM intake (kg)}}$

In Example 10, $M/D = \dfrac{168.7}{15} = 11.2$ MJ/kg DM

The results using equation (22) for dry matter intake values (Table 6), and the values for the ME allowances of cows (Table 4), to calculate minimum M/D values for rations, are given in Table 7.

Table 7—Minimum Metabolisable Energy concentrations of diets for cows, M/D (MJ/kg DM)

Breed and rate of liveweight change	Milk yield (kg/day)							
	0	5	10	15	20	25	30	35
JERSEY								
—0.5 kg/day	—	(5.9)	(8.6)	11.1	13.4			
No change	(4.6)	(7.5)	10.2	12.6				
+0.5 kg/day	—	(9.3)	11.8	14.1				
AYRSHIRE								
—0.5 kg/day	—	(5.0)	(6.7)	(8.3)	9.8	11.2	12.5	
No change	(4.3)	(6.1)	(7.8)	(9.4)	10.8	12.2	13.5	
+0.5 kg/day	—	(7.4)	(9.1)	10.6	12.0	13.3		
FRIESIAN								
—0.5 kg/day	—	(4.7)	(6.1)	(7.4)	(8.7)	9.8	10.9	12.0
No change	(4.2)	(5.7)	(7.1)	(8.4)	(9.6)	10.7	11.8	12.8
+0.5 kg/day	—	(6.8)	(8.1)	(9.4)	10.6	11.7	12.7	

( ) indicate theoretical values only as appetite limits on poor quality forage make rations infeasible.

If only silage (9 MJ/kg DM) and compound food (12.5 MJ/kg DM) are available, the weight of the two foods necessary to give an M/D of 11.2 MJ/kg can be calculated using the formula

$$FD = \frac{DMI\,(MC - M/D)}{(MC - MF)} \qquad (23)$$

where FD is forage dry matter intake, kg,

DMI is dry matter intake, kg,

MC is ME of compound food, MJ/kg DM

MF is ME of forage food, MJ/kg DM

In Example 10, $FD = \frac{15\,(12.5 - 11.2)}{(12.5 - 9)} = 5.6$ kg forage dry matter

Compound food dry matter intake, CD = DMI — FD = 15 — 5.6 = 9.4 kg DM
Thus a diet of 5.6 kg silage DM (28 kg silage as fed) and 9.4 kg compound food DM (10.9 kg cake as fed) will meet the cow's energy requirements.

Linear programming of dairy cow rations

Because of the additive nature of this ME system for dairy cows, linear programming using the ME values of foods is acceptable, subject to the application of total appetite constraints. Thus the ME values of foods define their replacement rates in dairy cattle rations, e.g. 1 kg barley DM (12.9 MJ/kg) will be replaced by 1.5 kg average hay DM (8.4 MJ/kg)

Such a replacement rate is markedly different from that given for the same foods by the starch equivalent system. This is due to the constant efficiency (k_1 = 0.62) with which food ME is used for lactation, compared with the widely varying efficiency with which food ME is used for fattening.

Feeding the dairy cow

Significance of liveweight changes
A typical 2 year old Friesian heifer after calving should weigh 450 kg, compared with a mature body weight by the 4th lactation of 600 kg. Thus growth to mature body size of about 40 kg per lactation must be allowed for in feeding programmes.

At parturition a cow loses a total of 60-70 kg liveweight comprising a calf of 40-50 kg birthweight and the associated tissues or afterbirth. Subsequently during the early weeks of lactation it is difficult to prevent further liveweight loss (mostly from fat reserves), this loss contributing to the cow's energy supply for lactation. This loss of liveweight should be regained during mid lactation and further growth allowed for (up to the 4th lactation) in addition to the requirements of pregnancy.

Evidence has accumulated that the scale of liveweight loss in cows in early lactation is related to the incidence of acetonaemia, low SNF in milk, and non-specific infertility, as well as reducing peak yield and thus lactation performance. It is suggested that in early lactation liveweight loss should be kept below 30 kg, or 0.5 kg per day.

In terms of liveweight gains or losses the following pattern during lactation is suggested as being both desirable and typical of well fed, high yielding cows.

Table B—Desirable pattern of liveweight change during lactation

Week number	Liveweight change, (kg/day)	Change during 10 weeks, (kg)	Net effect on liveweight, (kg)
1-10	− 0.5	− 35	− 35
11-20	0	0	− 35
21-30	+ 0.5	+ 35	0
31-40	+ 0.5	+ 35	+ 35
41-52	+ 0.75	+ 63	+ 98

Ration formulation for various stages of lactation
To show the consequence of this approach, consider the rations shown in Example 11.

Example 11
A Friesian cow weighing 600 kg has a yield of 23 kg/day at 2 weeks. Only silage, 9 MJ/kg DM, and compound food, 12.5 MJ/kg DM, are available.

First 10 weeks, early lactation
Calculation of peak yield
Peak yield (Y_p) is related to yield at 2 weeks (Y_2) by the formula

$$Y_p = 1.1\ Y_2\ \text{kg/day} \qquad (24)$$
Thus $Y_p = 1.1 \times 23 = 25$ kg/day

Alternatively probable peak yield can be estimated from the anticipated lactation milk yield of the cow divided by 200 i.e.,

$$Y_p = \frac{\text{Lactation yield (kg)}}{200} \text{ kg/day} \qquad (25)$$

In this example the anticipated yield in 305 days is 5,000 kg milk. Expected peak milk yield is therefore

$$Y_p = \frac{5000}{200} = 25 \text{ kg/day}$$

Probable dry matter appetite in early lactation

From equation (22), DMI = 0.025 W + 0.1 Y — 2.5*
= 15 + 2.5 — 2.5
= 15 kg DM/day

correction for early lactation

Maximum liveweight loss allowable = 0.5 kg/day

ME allowance can now be calculated:

M_m = 63 MJ		(Table 1)
M_p = 25 × 4.9 = 123 MJ		(Table 2)
M_g = — (0.5 × 28) = — 14 MJ		
ME allowance = 63 + 123 — 14 = 172 MJ/day		(Table 4)

$$M/D = \frac{172}{15} = 11.5 \text{ MJ/kg DM}$$

Using equation (23)

$$FD = \frac{15(12.5 - 11.5)}{(12.5 - 9)} = 4.3 \text{ kg DM forage}$$

CD = 15 — 4.3 = 10.7 kg DM compound food (12.6 kg as fed)

Thus the forage supplies 4.3 × 9 = 39 MJ, or two-thirds of the maintenance needs of the cow, whilst the compound food is fed at 0.5 kg/kg of milk. This amounts to *lead feeding* of 1.6 kg of compound food, equivalent to 3.6 kg of milk. Despite this lead feeding, the cow is losing 0.5 kg body weight daily, because of her restricted dry matter intake in early lactation.

Weeks 10-20, mid lactation

Peak milk yield of 25 kg will have been achieved and will begin to decline at about 2.5% each week. Liveweight loss should be brought to an end and dry matter appetite will be at its maximum.

Thus

M_m = 63 MJ
M_p = 123 MJ reducing to 99 MJ for 20 kg milk (Table 2)
M_g = 0
ME allowance = 63 + 123 = 186 reducing to 162 MJ
DMI = 0.025 W + 0.1 Y = 17.5 kg DM/day (Table 6)

$$M/D = \frac{186}{17.5} = 10.6 \text{ MJ/kg DM}$$

FD = 9.5 kg/day of forage DM
CD = 8.0 kg/day of compound food DM

The forage now supplies 9.5 × 9 = 86 MJ of ME daily, equivalent to maintenance and 4.7 kg of milk.

Feeding rates for feeding according to yield

Whilst there is evidence that feeding according to yield in the strictest sense is not really necessary, it is still a widespread method of deciding food allocations for cows. Feeding rates which are in accordance with the ME allowances of cows, assuming standard dairy compound food has an ME of 11 MJ/kg as fed, are as follows:

        Friesian milk   0.44 kg/kg milk
        Ayrshire milk   0.46 kg/kg milk
        Channel Island milk 0.54 kg/kg milk

0.44 kg/kg milk is equivalent to 4.5 lb/gallon milk.

Energy requirements of grazing dairy cows

Observations of cows at grass show that they are capable of gaining 1 kg/day or more in spring, as well as milking heavily, and that if they are to calve down in satisfactory condition, they will need to gain between 0.5 and 0.75 kg/day during the grazing season. Since 1 kg liveweight gain is equivalent to a dietary allowance of 34 MJ of ME, the energy requirement for an average gain of 0.5 kg/day over a grazing season of 150 days is 2,500 MJ, *equivalent to 250 kg grass DM.*

This substantial additional energy requirement of grazing cows is usually overlooked when calculating pasture outputs.

It follows that the first consequence on cows of a shortage of grazing is a reduction in liveweight gain rather than milk yield. Supplementary foods offered whilst cows are at grass affect liveweight gain before milk yield. In the long term this may be a sound decision, because cows can store surplus food energy and release it very efficiently during a subsequent period of dietary shortage.

Summary

ME system for dairy cows

Maintenance allowance

$$M_m = 8.3 + 0.091\,W \qquad \text{(Table 1a)}$$

(including activity allowance and a safety margin)

Milk production allowances

Energy value of milk: $EV_l = 0.0386\,BF + 0.0205\,SNF - 0.236$ (MJ/kg)
Energy secreted as milk: $E_l = EV_l \times Y$ (MJ)
Efficiency of ME utilisation for lactation: $k_l = 0.62$
ME allowance for milk produced: $M_l = 1.69\,E_l$ (MJ)   (Tables 2 and 3)
    (including safety margin)
ME for average milk (38 g/kg BF, 87 g/kg SNF) = 5.1 MJ/kg
ME for SCM milk (40 g/kg BF, 89 g/kg SNF) = 5.3 MJ/kg

Adjustments to energy allowances to allow for liveweight change in lactating cows

$$M_g = +\,34 \text{ MJ/kg gain}$$
$$M_g = -\,28 \text{ MJ/kg loss}$$

Section III—Use of the Metabolisable Energy system for growing and fattening cattle

The system provides a convenient method of predicting lightweight gain from a knowledge of ME intake and ME concentration of the ration. It is also possible to use it for the formulation of rations to give desired levels of performance.

Prediction of performance

It is convenient to consider the likely production from a given intake of ME for beef cattle in two separate stages—the energy allowance for maintenance and then the energy available for liveweight gain. To predict the expected liveweight gain from a given ration it is necessary to know the following:

(a) liveweight, W (kg)
(b) weights of individual foods given (kg/day)
(c) dry matter, DM (g/kg) and metabolisable energy (MJ/kg DM) contents of the foods

and to calculate:

(d) total ME supplied by the ration, MER (MJ/day)
(e) dry matter content of the ration, DMI (kg/day)
(f) energy concentration of the ration, M/D (MJ/kg/DM)
(g) ME allowance for maintenance, M_m (MJ/day)
(h) ME available for production, MEP (MJ/day)
(j) expected liveweight gain, LWG (kg/day)

Calculation of the total ME, DMI and M/D of the ration

The food dry matter and ME contributions are summed as shown in Example 10 (page 27). M/D is calculated from the expression

$$M/D = \frac{MER}{DMI}$$

Calculation of the ME allowance for maintenance

As indicated in Section I, the minimum net energy that must be available for maintenance is the fasting metabolism (FM) and may be calculated from the equation

$$FM = 5.67 + 0.061\ W \qquad (4)$$

Since no activity increment is considered necessary for beef cattle kept indoors, this represents the net energy for maintenance (E_m). Since the efficiency (k_m), with which ME is utilised for maintenance is 0.72, the ME requirement for maintenance, (M_m) is

$$\frac{FM}{0.72} = 1.39 \text{ FM}$$

Including a safety margin of 0.05, the ME allowance for maintenance, (M_m) becomes
$$M_m = 8.3 + 0.091 \text{ W} \tag{20}$$

Values of M_m for various liveweights are shown in Table 1b (see also page 22).

Table 1b—Daily maintenance allowance of ME for housed beef cattle

Body weight (kg)	MJ/head
100	17
150	22
200	27
250	31
300	36
350	40
400	45
450	49
500	54
550	59
600	63

(including safety margin)
Based on $M_m = 8.3 + 0.091$ W
(Note: The values are the same as those for dairy cattle but do not include an activity allowance).

Calculation of the ME available for production

The ME available for liveweight gain (MEP) is obtained by deducting the ME allowance for maintenance (M_m) from the total ME of the ration (MER):
$$\text{MEP} = \text{MER} - M_m \tag{26}$$

Calculation of predicted liveweight gain

The efficiency (k_g) with which MEP is utilised for gain, (as indicated in Section I) depends on the energy concentration, (M/D) of the ration
$$k_g = 0.0435 \text{ M/D} \tag{8}$$

Allowing a 0.05 safety margin, the net energy used for growth, (E_g) can be calculated from the expression:
$$E_g = \frac{\text{MEP} \times 0.0435 \text{ M/D}}{1.05}$$

$$= \text{MEP} \times 0.0414 \text{ M/D} \tag{27}$$

Values of E_g for various combinations of MEP and M/D are shown in Table 8.

Table 8—MJ net energy stored E_g, from ME available for production MEP, at energy concentration M/D

MEP (MJ)	\multicolumn{8}{c}{Energy concentration M/D, (MJ/kg DM)}
	7	8	9	10	11	12	13	14
5	1.4	1.7	1.9	2.1	2.3	2.5	2.7	2.9
10	2.9	3.3	3.7	4.1	4.6	5.0	5.4	5.8
15	4.3	5.0	5.6	6.2	6.8	7.5	8.1	8.7
20	5.8	6.6	7.5	8.3	9.1	9.9	10.8	11.6
25	7.2	8.3	9.3	10.4	11.4	12.4	13.5	14.5
30	8.7	9.9	11.2	12.4	13.7	14.9	16.1	17.4
35	10.1	11.6	13.0	14.5	15.9	17.4	18.8	20.3
40	11.6	13.2	14.9	16.6	18.2	19.9	21.5	23.2
45	13.0	14.9	16.8	18.6	20.5	22.4	24.2	26.1
50	14.5	16.6	18.6	20.7	22.8	24.8	26.9	29.0
55	15.9	18.2	20.5	22.8	25.0	27.3	29.6	31.9
60	17.4	19.9	22.4	24.8	27.3	29.8	32.3	34.8
65	18.8	21.5	24.2	26.9	29.6	32.3	35.0	37.7
70	20.3	23.2	26.1	29.0	31.9	34.8	37.7	40.6
75	21.7	24.8	27.9	31.1	34.2	37.3	40.4	43.5
80	23.2	26.5	29.8	33.1	36.4	39.8	43.1	46.4

Based on $E_g = MEP \times 0.0414$ M/D

The liveweight gain (LWG) that can be achieved from the stored energy (E_g) as shown in Section I, is dependent upon the energy value of the gain (EV_g), which in turn is related to the liveweight of the animal (W) and the net energy stored as gain (E_g). These relationships can be expressed as equation (9) discussed in Section I (page 15). The equation is:

$$LWG = \frac{E_g}{(6.28 + 0.3\, E_g + 0.0188\, W)} \qquad (9)$$

The liveweight gains possible from various levels of energy stored, (E_g) for different liveweights (W) are given in Table 9.

Below are some example calculations for predicting liveweight gains from given rations.

Example 12
Prediction of expected liveweight gain of a 250 kg steer receiving the following daily ration:

	DMI (kg)	ME (MJ)
4.1 kg hay (870 g/kg DM, 9 MJ/kg DM)	3.6	32.1
1.7 kg barley (840 g/kg DM, 12.5 MJ/kg DM)	1.4	17.9
	5.0	50.0

Total ME of ration, MER = 50 MJ/day

Hence the ration energy concentration M/D = $\frac{50}{5.0}$ = 10 MJ/kg DM

Reference to Table 1b shows that for a liveweight of 250 kg, 31 MJ of ME will be needed for maintenance (M_m). Therefore,

$$\text{ME available for production (MEP)} = \text{MER} - M_m \quad (26)$$
$$= 50 - 31$$
$$= 19 \text{ MJ at M/D 10 MJ/kg DM}$$
$$\text{Net energy stored } E_g = \text{MEP} \times 0.0414 \text{ M/D} \quad \text{(Table 8)}$$
$$= 19 \times 0.0414 \times 10 \text{ MJ}$$
$$= 7.9 \text{ MJ}$$

Using equation (9), from Table 9, it will be seen that the liveweight gain possible for a 250 kg steer from a net energy (E_g) of 7.9 MJ is 0.6 kg per day.

Table 9—Liveweight gain in kg/day for MJ Net Energy stored E_g, in animals of liveweight W

E_g (MJ)	Liveweight W(kg)										
	100	150	200	250	300	350	400	450	500	550	600
2	0.23	0.21	0.19	0.17	0.16	0.15	0.14	0.13	0.12	0.12	0.11
4	0.43	0.39	0.36	0.33	0.30	0.28	0.27	0.25	0.24	0.22	0.21
6	0.60	0.55	0.51	0.47	0.44	0.41	0.38	0.36	0.34	0.33	0.31
8	0.76	0.70	0.64	0.60	0.56	0.52	0.49	0.47	0.44	0.42	0.40
10	0.90	0.83	0.77	0.72	0.67	0.63	0.60	0.56	0.54	0.51	0.49
12	1.02	0.94	0.88	0.82	0.77	0.73	0.69	0.65	0.62	0.59	0.57
14		1.05	0.98	0.92	0.87	0.82	0.78	0.74	0.70	0.67	0.64
16			1.08	1.01	0.96	0.91	0.86	0.82	0.78	0.75	0.72
18			1.17	1.10	1.04	0.99	0.94	0.89	0.85	0.82	0.78
20				1.18	1.12	1.06	1.01	0.96	0.92	0.88	0.85
22				1.25	1.19	1.13	1.08	1.03	0.99	0.95	0.91
24					1.26	1.20	1.14	1.09	1.05	1.01	0.97
26					1.32	1.26	1.20	1.15	1.11	1.06	1.03
28						1.32	1.26	1.21	1.16	1.12	1.08
30						1.37	1.32	1.26	1.22	1.17	1.13
35							1.44	1.39	1.34	1.29	1.25
40								1.50	1.45	1.40	1.35
45									1.54	1.49	1.45
50										1.58	1.54

$$\text{Based on LWG} = \frac{E_g}{(6.28 + 0.3 \, E_g + 0.0188 \, W)}$$

Example 13

Calculation of the predicted liveweight gain of a 235 kg steer fed a daily ration of

	DMI (kg)	ME (MJ)
9.5 kg silage (217 g/kg DM, 8.8 MJ/kg DM)	2.06	18.1
7.5 kg potatoes (270 g/kg DM, 11.2 MJ/kg DM)	2.03	22.7
2.5 kg barley (870 g/kg DM, 12.5 MJ/kg DM)	2.18	27.2
	6.27	68.0

hence $M/D = \dfrac{68.0}{6.27} = 10.85$ MJ/kg DM

$M_m = 30$ MJ (Table 1b)
MEP $= 68.0 - 30 = 38$ MJ at 10.85 MJ/kg DM
$E_g = 17.1$ (Table 8)
LWG $= 1.08$ kg/day (Table 9)

The ration supplies 68 MJ at M/D 10.85 MJ/kg DM and will provide for maintenance and 1.1 kg liveweight gain per day.

Calculation of Metabolisable Energy allowances

To calculate the dietary ME allowances needed by growing and fattening cattle, it is necessary to know the following:
(a) animal's liveweight, W, (kg)
(b) desired rate of daily liveweight gain, LWG (kg/day)
(c) energy concentration of the ration, M/D (MJ/kg DM)

and to calculate:
(d) ME maintenance allowance, M_m, (MJ/day)
(e) energy stored as gain, E_g (MJ/day)
(f) ME allowance for body gain, M_g (MJ/day)
(g) total ME allowance (MJ/day)

These calculations are made using the following equations:

Maintenance allowance, $M_m = 8.3 + 0.091\ W$ (20)

$$\text{Energy stored, } E_g = \dfrac{LWG\,(6.28 + 0.0188\ W)}{(1 - 0.30\ LWG)} \quad (7)$$

ME for body gain $M_g = \dfrac{E_g}{k_g}$

Using equation (8) for k_g with a safety margin of 0.05:

$$M_g = \dfrac{E_g}{0.0414\ M/D} = \dfrac{24.1 E_g}{M/D} \quad (27a)$$

which is a rearranged version of equation (27) on page 34.

Total ME allowance (MJ/day) $= M_m + M_g$

Calculated ME allowances for growing and fattening beef cattle from 100 to 600 kg liveweight and gaining up to 1.5 kg/day are given in Table 10.

Inspection of Table 10 shows that the ME allowances for beef cattle vary according to the energy concentration of the ration (M/D), when a particular rate of gain is required. The ME of a poorer food such as hay (M/D = 8) is used less efficiently for gain than cereals such as barley (M/D = 13). This is a consequence of the effect of M/D on k_g as given in equation (8).

This interaction between the energy concentration of the ration and the ME allowance leads to some difficulty in ration formulation for beef cattle, but several methods can be used to solve this problem.

Table 10—Daily ME allowances for growing and fattening cattle (MJ/day)

Liveweight (kg)	Ration M/D (MJ/kg DM)	\multicolumn{7}{c}{Rate of gain (kg/day)}						
		0	0.25	0.50	0.75	1.00	1.25	1.50
100	8	17	24					
	10	17	22	29				
	12	17	21	27	33			
	14	17	21	25	31	37		
150	8	22	29					
	10	22	28	35				
	12	22	27	33	40	48		
	14	22	26	31	37	44	53	
200	8	27	35					
	10	27	34	41	51			
	12	27	33	39	47	56		
	14	27	32	37	45	52	62	74
250	8	31	40	51				
	10	31	38	47	57			
	12	31	37	44	52	63	75	
	14	31	36	42	49	58	69	83
300	8	36	46	57				
	10	36	44	53	64			
	12	36	43	50	59	70	84	
	14	36	42	48	56	65	77	92
350	8	40	51	63				
	10	40	48	58	70	84		
	12	40	47	55	65	77	92	
	14	40	46	53	62	72	84	101
400	8	45	56	70				
	10	45	54	65	77	93		
	12	45	53	61	72	85	101	
	14	45	51	59	68	79	93	110
450	8	49	61	75				
	10	49	59	70	83			
	12	49	57	67	78	91	108	
	14	49	56	64	74	85	100	118
500	8	54	67	82				
	10	54	64	76	91			
	12	54	63	73	85	99	117	
	14	54	61	70	80	93	108	128
550	8	59	73	89				
	10	59	70	83	98			
	12	59	68	79	91	107	126	
	14	59	67	76	87	100	116	137
600	8	63	77	94				
	10	63	75	88	104			
	12	63	73	84	97	114	134	
	14	63	71	81	92	106	124	146

Formulation of a ration to give a desired level of production

To formulate a ration to allow a desired rate of liveweight gain it is necessary to know the following:
- (a) liveweight of the animal, W (kg)
- (b) liveweight gain required, LWG (kg/day)
- (c) ME content of the available foods, MEF (MJ/kg DM)
- (d) dry matter content of the available foods, DM (g/kg)
- (e) estimated dry matter appetite of the animal (kg/day)

and to calculate:
- (f) ME allowance for maintenance, M_m (MJ/day)
- (g) net energy allowance for production, E_g (MJ/day)
- (h) range of ME required for production, M_g (MJ/day)

The value of energy stored (E_g) for a particular rate of gain will enable the ME required for production (M_g), to be calculated for the range of energy concentrations (M/D) of the foods available.

Example 14

Ration formulation for a steer of 250 kg liveweight required to gain 0.8 kg/day.
The foods available are hay and compound food:

Hay	(850 g/kg DM, 8 MJ/kg DM)	
Compound food	(880 g/kg DM, 12.5 MJ/kg DM)	
Dry matter appetite,	DMI = 6.6 kg/day	
Maintenance ME allowance, M_m	= 31 MJ/day	(Table 1)
Net energy allowance for production, E_g	= 11.6 MJ/day	(Table 9)

The range of M/D values to be considered for predicting the ME for production is from 8.0 MJ/kg DM for the hay to 12.5 MJ/kg DM for the compound food. Inspection of Table 8 shows that for a value for E_g of 12 MJ, values for M_g will be between 24 and 36 MJ for the energy concentrations available in the foods.
Since M_m = 31 MJ, the total ME allowance will be in the range 55-67 MJ/day.

First attempted solution

		DMI (kg)	ME (MJ)
6 kg hay,	(850 g/kg DM, 8 MJ/kg DM)	5.1	40.8
1.5 kg compound,	(880 g/kg DM, 12.5 MJ/kg DM)	1.3	16.5
		6.4	57.3

$$M/D = 8.95 \text{ MJ/kg DM}$$
$$MEP = 57.3 - 31 = 26.3 \text{ MJ/day}$$
$$E_g = 26.3 \times 0.0414 \times 8.95 \text{ MJ/day}$$
$$= 9.7 \text{ MJ/day compared with } 11.6 \text{ MJ/day required}$$

Second attempted solution

		DMI (kg)	ME (MJ)
5 kg hay,	(850 g/kg DM, 8 MJ/kg DM)	4.25	34.0
2.5 kg compound,	(880 g/kg DM, 12.5 MJ/kg DM)	2.20	27.5
		6.45	61.5

M/D = 9.5 MJ/kg DM
MEP = 61.5 − 31 = 30.5 MJ/day
E_g = 12.0 MJ/day compared with 11.6 MJ/day required

This may be regarded as a close enough approximation for practical purposes, but is obviously not the exact solution which is

		DMI (kg)	ME (MJ)
5.5 kg hay,	(850 g/kg DM, 8 MJ/kg DM)	4.68	37.4
2.15 kg compound,	(880 g/kg DM, 12.5 MJ/kg DM)	1.89	23.6
		6.57	61.0

M/D = 9.3 MJ/kg DM
MEP = 61 − 31 = 30 MJ/day
E_g = 11.6 MJ/day equal to a gain of 0.8 kg/day

Thus a ration consisting of 5.5 kg hay DM and 2.15 kg compound food DM will supply 61 MJ of ME at a ration concentration of 9.3 MJ/kg DM and will provide for 0.8 kg gain per day in a 250 kg steer.

A rapid method of ration formulation

The foregoing iterative method of calculation is slow and laborious, and a more satisfactory procedure will now be outlined, which gives the exact answer directly, provided that dry matter appetite of the animal can be specified.

By definition, ME intake = Dry matter intake × M/D
or MER = DMI × M/D
and ideally ration ME (MER) should be equal to $M_m + M_g$

$$M_m = 8.3 + 0.091\ W \tag{20}$$

$$M_g = \frac{24.1\ E_g}{M/D} \tag{27a}$$

Equating the two expressions for MER,

$$DMI \times M/D = M_m + \frac{24.1\ E_g}{M/D} \tag{28}$$

All the terms in equation (28) are known, being directly related either to liveweight (W) (Table 1b), or to liveweight gain (Table 9). Roy's (1959)[1] values for dry matter intakes may be used.

Equation (28) can be solved by multiplying throughout by M/D and rearranging the components.

$$DMI \times (M/D)^2 = M_m \times M/D + 24.1\ E_g$$
$$DMI \times (M/D)^2 - (M_m \times M/D) - 24.1\ E_g = 0 \tag{29}$$

This is an equation in quadratic form and may be written as

$$ax^2 + bx + c = 0$$

where a = DMI, x = M/D, b = − M_m , c = − 24.1 E_g

---

[1] Proceedings of the Brighton Conference, 1959

The solution for x is given by the formula
$$x = \frac{-b \pm \sqrt{(b^2 - 4ac)}}{2a}$$

The only feasible solution to equation (29) is:
$$M/D = \frac{M_m + \sqrt{[M_m^2 + (96.4\ DMI \times E_g)]}}{2DMI} \quad (30)$$

From equation (30) can be calculated the exact energy concentration (M/D) which satisfies both the animal's dry matter appetite and its need for ME for maintenance and liveweight gain. Calculated values are given in Table 11 (page 43).

The use of this concept of minimum M/D values for rations is the key to simple ration formulation in the ME system.

Two component rations If the ration consists of only two components, forage and supplement, the amounts of the two foods required may be calculated as for dairy cattle using equation (23):

$$FD, \quad \text{forage dry matter intake} = \frac{DMI\ (MC - M/D)}{(MC - MF)} \quad \text{kg/day (23)}$$

and CD, cereal/compound food dry matter = DMI — FD kg/day

where MF is the ME of forage DM

MC is the ME of cereals or compound food DM

M/D is the appropriate value in Table 11

and DMI is the dry matter appetite given in Table 11.

Example 15
Formulation of a ration for a 300 kg steer to gain 1.0 kg/day. Foods available are forage (ME = 9 MJ/kg/DM) and compound food (ME = 12 MJ/kg DM).
  From Table 11, minimum M/D = 10.0 MJ/kg DM and DMI = 7.62 kg/day
      forage ME, MF = 9 MJ/kg DM
  and compound food ME, MC = 12 MJ/kg DM
Then using equation (23):
$$FD = \frac{7.62\ (12 - 10)}{(12 - 9)} = 5.08\ \text{kg DM/day}$$
  and CD = 7.62 — 5.08 = 2.54 kg DM/day

Hence the desired ration is 5.08 kg forage DM and 2.54 kg compound food DM.

The ration formulation equation (23), for calculating weight of forage dry matter required for a given energy concentration (M/D), will handle only a two component ration. A little ingenuity, however, can be used to handle more foods, if they can be grouped and proportioned so that the mixture can be given an ME value.

For example,

given hay at 8 MJ/kg DM
and silage at 10 MJ/kg DM
} fed in equal proportions,

the mix would have an ME value of 9 MJ which can be inserted as MF in equation (23).

Normally, however, if a variety of foods is to be included in a ration and economic considerations taken into account, the use of the linear programming technique is desirable.

Linear programming of rations for beef animals

It should now be apparent that the ME value of a food does not accurately represent its contribution to animal production, since the efficiency of utilisation of the ME for liveweight gain (k_g), is influenced by the energy concentration (M/D), and therefore by the other foods in the ration.

Diets for pigs and poultry are commonly formulated to specified energy concentrations (M/D), whilst complete diets for dairy cattle are formulated to give a specified daily allowance of ME(MER). With beef cattle, the ration must be defined by both terms, total MER and energy concentration (M/D); linear programming using MER alone as the energy constraint is unsound. The right hand side of the matrix must have values for both total ME and the chosen energy concentration (M/D). Alternatively a statement of dry matter intake (DMI) required can be used instead of M/D, since MER = DMI × M/D.

The break-even prices and substitution rates which can be calculated for rations for low rates of gain will differ substantially from those found when rations for high rates of gain are formulated.

An alternative approach is to use the variable net energy system described in the following section.

Variable Net Energy system for ration formulation

This system is based on principles put forward by MacHardy (1965)[1], and worked out in detail by Harkins, Edwards and McDonald (1974)[2]. It calculates the net energy for each food at the level of animal production under study, thus making the system additive, and ideal for use in linear programme work. Replacement rates can be calculated for any situation, and it is of great value in desk formulation of multi feed rations without recourse either to linear programming or the use of equation (30) described earlier.

The system states allowances in net energy and is based on two concepts, Animal Production Level (APL), and Net Energy for maintenance and production (NE$_{mp}$), which were discussed at the end of Section I. For any given animal production level a food has a net energy dependent upon its metabolisable energy concentration. Tables may be constructed which allow the net energy (NE$_{mp}$) values to be obtained if the production situation and metabolisable energy values (MEF) of the foods are known.

Abst. 9th Int Cong. Anim. Prod., p25. [2]Anim. Prod. **19**, 141, 1974

Table 11—Minimum metabolisable energy concentration of beef cattle diets, M/D (MJ/kg DM) at stated levels of dry matter intake DMI (kg/day)

Gain (kg/day)	Liveweight W(kg)									
	100	150	200	250	300	350	400	450	500	550	600
0	(5.8)	(5.2)	(4.8)	(4.7)	(4.6)	(4.7)	(4.8)	(4.9)	(5.1)	(5.3)	(5.4)
0.1	(6.8)	(6.0)	(5.5)	(5.4)	(5.3)	(5.4)	(5.5)	(5.5)	(5.7)	(5.9)	(6.0)
0.2	7.6	(6.8)	(6.2)	(6.1)	(5.9)	(6.0)	(6.0)	(6.1)	(6.2)	(6.4)	(6.6)
0.3	8.4	7.5	(6.9)	(6.7)	(6.5)	(6.5)	(6.6)	(6.6)	(6.8)	7.0	7.1
0.4	9.1	8.1	7.5	7.2	7.0	7.0	7.1	7.1	7.3	7.5	7.6
0.5	9.8	8.7	8.0	7.8	7.5	7.5	7.6	7.6	7.7	7.9	8.1
0.6	10.5	9.3	8.5	8.3	8.1	8.0	8.0	8.1	8.2	8.4	8.5
0.7	11.1	9.8	9.1	8.8	8.5	8.5	8.5	8.5	8.7	8.8	9.0
0.8	11.8	10.4	9.6	9.3	9.0	9.0	9.0	9.0	9.1	9.3	9.5
0.9	12.5	11.0	10.1	9.8	9.5	9.4	9.5	9.5	9.6	9.8	9.9
1.0	13.1	11.6	10.7	10.3	10.0	9.9	9.9	9.9	10.1	10.2	10.4
1.1	13.8	12.1	11.2	10.8	10.5	10.4	10.4	10.4	10.6	10.7	10.9
1.2	14.5	12.8	11.8	11.3	11.0	10.9	10.9	10.9	11.1	11.2	11.4
1.3		13.4	12.4	11.9	11.6	11.5	11.4	11.4	11.6	11.7	11.9
1.4		14.0	13.0	12.5	12.1	12.0	12.0	12.0	12.1	12.3	12.5
1.5			13.6	13.1	12.7	12.6	12.5	12.5	12.7	12.9	13.0
DMI (kg/day)	2.94	4.26	5.48	6.60	7.62	8.54	9.36	10.08	10.70	11.22	11.65

( ) indicates values are theoretical only, appetite limits on poor quality forages make M/D infeasible.

Based on $M/D = \dfrac{M_m + \sqrt{M_m^2 + (96.4\ DMI \times E_g)}}{2\ DMI}$

Animal Production Level

This is defined as the ratio between the total net energy requirement and the net energy required for maintenance (E_m):

$$\text{Animal Production Level, APL} = \frac{E_m + E_p}{E_m} = 1 + \frac{E_p}{E_m} \quad (19)$$

$$\text{Given that } E_m = 5.67 + 0.061\ W \quad (4)$$

$$\text{and } E_p = \frac{LWG\ (6.28 + 0.0188\ W)}{(1 - 0.3\ LWG)} \quad (7)$$

then for this energy system,

$$APL = 1 + \left[\frac{LWG\ (6.28 + 0.0188\ W)}{(1 - 0.3\ LWG)\ (5.67 + 0.061\ W)}\right] \quad (31)$$

Values for APL at different levels of liveweight (W), and liveweight gain (LWG), are stated in Table 12. At maintenance level, when LWG = 0, APL = 1.

Table 12—Animal Production Level (APL)

Liveweight W, (kg)	Liveweight gain LWG, (kg/day)					
	0.25	0.50	0.75	1.00	1.25	1.50
100	1.19	1.40	1.66	1.98		
150	1.16	1.36	1.59	1.87		
200	1.15	1.33	1.54	1.79	2.11	
250	1.14	1.30	1.50	1.74	2.03	
300	1.13	1.29	1.47	1.70	1.97	2.33
350	1.13	1.27	1.45	1.67	1.93	2.27
400	1.12	1.26	1.43	1.64	1.90	2.22
450	1.12	1.26	1.42	1.62	1.87	2.18
500	1.11	1.25	1.41	1.60	1.84	2.15
550	1.11	1.24	1.40	1.59	1.83	2.13
600	1.11	1.24	1.39	1.58	1.81	2.13

$$\text{Based on APL} = 1 + \left[\frac{\text{LWG } (6.28 + 0.0188W)}{(1 - 0.3 \text{ LWG})(5.67 + 0.061 W)} \right]$$

Net Energy for maintenance and production

In the ME system for beef cattle the efficiency of utilisation of ME for maintenance (k_m) is fixed at 0.72, and the efficiency for fattening (k_g) is dependent on the ration energy concentration (M/D).

$$k_g = 0.0435 \text{ M/D} \tag{8}$$

Overall efficiency of ME use for maintenance and production (k_{mp}) is therefore variable, depending on the proportions of ME used for maintenance and fattening. It may be defined as the ratio of net energy requirement for maintenance and production, to the total metabolisable energy requirement (M_{mp}):

$$k_{mp} = \frac{E_m + E_p}{M_{mp}} \tag{18}$$

$$\text{and } M_{mp} = M_m + M_p$$

$$\text{Hence } k_{mp} = \frac{E_m + E_p}{M_m + M_p} \tag{32}$$

Using the general expression $ME = \frac{NE}{k}$,

Metabolisable energy required for maintenance, $M_m = \frac{E_m}{0.72} = 1.39 \, E_m$

Given that $APL = \frac{E_m + E_p}{E_m}$, then $E_p = E_m \, (APL - 1)$

Metabolisable energy required for production $M_p = \frac{E_p}{0.0435 \text{ M/D}} \tag{8}$

$$= \frac{E_m \, (APL - 1)}{0.0435 \text{ M/D}}$$

Substituting for E_p, M_m and M_p in terms of E_m, M/D or APL in equation (32) the following expression is obtained:

$$k_{mp} = \frac{M/D \times APL}{1.39 \, M/D + 23 \, (APL - 1)} \quad (33)$$

Thus the overall efficiency of ME use (k_{mp}) can be calculated for any given animal production level and energy concentration of the ration, as may be seen in the following table:

Table C—Overall efficiency of ME utilisation, k_{mp}

APL	Ration energy concentration, M/D (MJ/kg DM)						
	8	9	10	11	12	13	14
1.00	0.72	0.72	0.72	0.72	0.72	0.72	0.72
1.25	0.59	0.62	0.64	0.65	0.67	0.68	0.69
1.50	0.53	0.56	0.59	0.62	0.64	0.66	0.68
1.75	0.49	0.53	0.56	0.59	0.62	0.64	0.67
2.00	0.47	0.51	0.54	0.58	0.61	0.63	0.66
2.25	0.45	0.49	0.53	0.56	0.59	0.62	0.65

Net Energy values of foods

The net energy for maintenance and production, (NE_{mp}) of either a ration or a food can be obtained by multiplying the ME concentration in the dry matter, (M/D or MEF) by k_{mp}. If equation (33) is multiplied by MEF, then:

$$NE_{mp} = \frac{(MEF)^2 \times APL}{1.39 \, MEF + 23 \, (APL - 1)} \quad (MJ/kg\,DM) \quad (34)$$

The net energies calculated using this equation are stated in Table 13.

Any production situation may be defined in terms of APL (Table 12), and NE_{mp} values found by reference to Table 13 (page 47).

Net Energy allowances for beef cattle

The formulation of rations using the NE_{mp} values of foods requires net energy allowances calculated in the same unit. These can be obtained by using equations for E_m and E_p already referred to:

$$E_m = 5.67 + 0.061 \, W \quad (4)$$

$$\text{and } E_p = \frac{LWG \, (6.28 + 0.0188 \, W)}{(1 - 0.3 \, LWG)} \quad (7)$$

These values must be increased by the usual 0.05 safety margin as has been done with other systems. Total net energy allowances for maintenance and gain are given in Table 14 (page 47).

Use of the variable Net Energy system for ration formulation

Within dry matter appetite limits, rations for beef animals can be constructed in an additive manner by using the appropriate NE_{mp} values for the desired animal production level. In order to do this, it is necessary to know the following:

(a) animal's liveweight, W (kg)
(b) required rate of liveweight gain, LWG (kg/day)
(c) expected dry matter intake, DMI (kg/day)
(d) foods dry matter content, DM (g/kg)
   and ME content, MEF (MJ/kg DM)

and to calculate

(e) animal production level, APL
(f) net energy allowance for maintenance and gain (MJ/day)
(g) appropriate NE_{mp} values for each food (MJ/kg DM)

and to formulate a ration which meets the values in (f) and (c)

The following examples illustrate the use of the Net Energy system in ration formulation for beef cattle.

Example 16
Formulation of a ration for a 400 kg steer to gain 0.5 kg/day

Foods available: Hay MEF 8 MJ/kg DM
Cereal MEF 13 MJ/kg DM

APL =	1.26	(Table 12)
NE_{mp} of hay =	4.7 MJ/kg DM	(Table 13)
NE_{mp} of cereal =	8.9 MJ/kg DM	(Table 13)
Net energy requirement =	40.1 MJ/day	(Table 14)

Daily ration

	DMI (kg)	NE (MJ)
6.6 kg hay DM at 4.7 MJ/kg DM	6.6	31.0
1 kg cereal DM at 8.9 MJ/kg DM	1.0	8.9
	7.6	39.9

Thus, a daily ration of 6.6 kg hay DM and 1.0 kg cereal DM will supply 39.9 MJ net energy and produce 0.5 kg liveweight gain per day in a 400 kg steer. This diet is well within the limit of dry matter intake given in Table 11.

Example 17
A 250 kg steer is required to gain 0.75 kg/day.
There is sufficient hay to feed 6 kg/day. How much cereal should be fed in addition?

Dry matter intake, DMI = 6.5 kg/day		(Table 11)
Foods available: Hay (850 g/kg DM, MEF 8 MJ/kg DM)		
Cereal (860 g/kg DM, MEF 13 MJ/kg DM)		
APL = 1.50		(Table 12)
Net Energy required = 33.2 MJ/day		(Table 14)

At APL 1.5 { Hay NE_{mp} = 4.2 MJ/kg DM (Table 13)
            { Cereal NE_{mp} = 8.6 MJ/kg DM (Table 13)

Daily ration

	DMI (kg)	NE (MJ)
6 kg hay, (850 g/kg DM, 4.2 MJ/kg DM)	5.1	21.4
1.6 kg cereal, (860 g/kg DM, 8.6 MJ/kg DM)	1.4	11.8
	6.5	33.2

Thus 1.6 kg cereal are required in addition to the 6 kg of hay to produce the required liveweight gain.

Table 13—Net Energies of foods for maintenance and production, NE$_{mp}$ (MJ/kg DM)

APL	ME of food, MEF (MJ/kg DM)								
	6	7	8	9	10	11	12	13	14
1.00	4.3	5.0	5.8	6.5	7.2	7.9	8.6	9.4	10.1
1.10	3.7	4.5	5.2	6.0	6.8	7.6	8.3	9.1	9.9
1.15	3.5	4.3	5.1	5.8	6.6	7.4	8.2	9.0	9.8
1.20	3.3	4.1	4.9	5.7	6.5	7.3	8.1	8.9	9.8
1.25	3.2	4.0	4.7	5.5	6.4	7.2	8.0	8.9	9.7
1.30	3.1	3.8	4.6	5.4	6.3	7.1	7.9	8.8	9.7
1.35	3.0	3.7	4.5	5.3	6.2	7.0	7.8	8.7	9.6
1.40	2.9	3.6	4.4	5.2	6.1	6.9	7.8	8.7	9.6
1.45	2.8	3.5	4.3	5.1	6.0	6.8	7.7	8.6	9.5
1.50	2.7	3.5	4.2	5.1	5.9	6.8	7.7	8.6	9.5
1.55	2.7	3.4	4.2	5.0	5.8	6.7	7.6	8.5	9.5
1.65	2.6	3.3	4.1	4.9	5.7	6.6	7.5	8.4	9.4
1.75	2.5	3.2	3.9	4.8	5.6	6.5	7.4	8.4	9.3
2.00	2.3	3.0	3.8	4.6	5.4	6.3	7.3	8.2	9.2
2.25	2.2	2.9	3.6	4.4	5.3	6.2	7.1	8.1	9.1

Based on NE$_{mp}$ = $\dfrac{(MEF)^2 \times APL}{1.39\ MEF + 23\ (APL - 1)}$

Table 14—Net Energy allowances (MJ/day) for maintenance and liveweight gain in growing and fattening animals

Gain (kg)	Liveweight, W (kg)									
	100	150	200	250	300	350	400	450	500	550	600
0	12.4	15.6	18.8	22.0	25.2	28.4	31.6	34.8	38.0	41.2	44.4
0.1	13.3	16.6	19.9	23.2	26.5	29.8	33.1	36.4	39.7	43.0	46.3
0.2	14.2	17.6	21.0	24.5	27.9	31.3	34.7	38.1	41.5	44.9	48.3
0.3	15.2	18.8	22.3	25.8	29.3	32.9	36.4	39.9	43.4	47.0	50.5
0.4	16.3	19.9	23.6	27.2	30.9	34.5	38.2	41.8	45.5	49.1	52.8
0.5	17.4	21.2	25.0	28.8	32.6	36.3	40.1	43.9	47.7	51.5	55.2
0.6	18.7	22.6	26.5	30.4	34.4	38.3	42.2	46.1	50.2	54.0	57.9
0.7	20.0	24.2	28.1	32.2	36.3	40.4	44.4	48.5	52.6	56.7	60.7
0.8	21.4	25.7	29.9	34.1	38.4	42.6	46.9	51.1	55.3	59.6	63.8
0.9	23.0	27.4	31.8	36.2	40.6	45.0	49.5	53.9	58.3	62.7	67.1
1.0	24.6	29.3	33.9	38.5	43.1	47.7	52.3	56.9	61.5	66.1	70.7
1.1		31.3	36.1	40.9	45.7	50.6	55.4	60.2	65.0	69.9	74.7
1.2			38.6	43.6	48.7	53.7	58.8	63.8	68.9	73.9	79.0
1.3				46.6	51.9	57.2	62.5	67.8	73.1	78.4	83.7
1.4					55.4	61.0	66.6	72.2	77.7	83.3	88.9
1.5						65.2	71.1	77.0	82.9	88.8	94.7

(including safety margin)

Based on NE allowance = E$_m$ + E$_g$, where
E$_m$ = 1.05 [5.67 + 0.061 W]
and E$_g$ = 1.05 $\left[\dfrac{LWG\ (6.28 + 0.0188\ W)}{(1 - 0.3\ LWG)} \right]$

Rapid ration formulation using the variable Net Energy system

To formulate rapidly a ration from two components only within the animal's expected dry matter intake, a minimum net energy concentration of the ration can be calculated from the net energy requirement and the probable dry matter intake, e.g., using the data in Example 17,

Minimum net energy concentration, $N/D = \dfrac{33.2}{6.5} = 5.11$ MJ/kg DM

A revised version of equation (23) can now be used, in which
$\quad$ M/D is replaced by N/D
$\quad$ MF by NE_{mp} of forage, NF
$\quad$ and MC by NE_{mp} of compound food, NC

Thus forage dry matter, $FD = \dfrac{DMI\,(NC - N/D)}{(NC - NF)}$ kg $\qquad(35)$

Continuing with Example 17

$FD = \dfrac{6.5\,(8.6 - 5.11)}{(8.6 - 4.2)} = 5.16$ kg DM

and CD = 6.5 — 5.16 = 1.34 kg DM

A daily ration consisting of 6.1 kg of hay as fed (5.16 kg DM) and 1.6 kg of cereal as fed (1.34 kg DM) should give the required rate of gain and does not exceed the limit of dry matter intake stated in Table 11.

Replacement values of foods for growing and fattening cattle

The relative values of foods are important when making decisions on their purchase or substitution in beef cattle rations. The variable net energy system provides an easy method for assessing the relative value of foods in a defined production situation.

Example 18

Calculation of the replacement value of two foods.

At APL 1.25
Feed A, of MEF 10 MJ/kg DM has a NE_{mp} value of 6.4 MJ/kg DM
Feed B, of MEF 14 MJ/kg DM has a NE_{mp} value of 9.7 MJ/kg DM $\quad$ (Table 13)

Hence $\dfrac{9.7}{6.4}$ kg DM of Feed A, i.e. 1.5 kg will replace 1 kg DM of Feed B in a fattening ration at an APL of 1.25.

At APL 1.75
Feed A has a NE_{mp} of 5.6 MJ/kg DM and Feed B, a NE_{mp} of 9.3 MJ/kg DM.
Thus $\dfrac{9.3}{5.6} = 1.7$ kg DM of Feed A are required to replace 1 kg DM of Feed B.

Linear programming of beef cattle rations using the variable Net Energy system

The matrix required for this purpose will have a number of entries under each food, of NE_{mp} values for each APL level chosen, as in Table 13. Thus rows of NE_{mp} values will be set up, each of which can only be used for net energy allowances from Table 14, at that APL value. Substitution rates and break-even prices will vary according to the APL chosen. It is suggested that APL = 1.25

could be used for rates of gain of 0.5kg/day and below, and APL = 1.60 for high rates of gain, about 1 kg/day, but this will lead to some loss of precision.

The usual dry matter appetite constraints should, of course, be used.

Final note

The variable net energy system **cannot be used to predict animal performance,** since the animal's liveweight gain must be known in order to calculate APL and hence NE_{mp} values. The ME system must be used for performance prediction as previously described.

Summary

ME system for beef cattle
Maintenance allowance with no allowance for activity:
(including safety margin)
$$M_m = 8.3 + 0.091\ W \quad \text{(Table 1b)}$$

Production allowances
ME available for production: MEP = MER − M_m
Efficiency of ME utilisation k_g = 0.0435 M/D
 for gain:

Net energy stored: E_g = MEP × k_g
Allowing for 0.05 safety
 margin this becomes: E_g = 0.0414 M/D × MEP (Table 8)
Energy value of gain: EV_g = 6.28 + 0.3 E_g + 0.0188 W
Predicted liveweight gain, LWG = $\dfrac{E_g}{EV_g}$

$$= \frac{E_g}{(6.28 + 0.3\ E_g + 0.0188\ W)}$$

(Table 9)

Variable Net Energy system for ration formulation for beef cattle

Net Energy for maintenance
(including safety margin) E_m = 1.05 [5.67 + 0.061 W]   (Table 14)

Net Energy for liveweight gain
(including safety margin) $E_p = 1.05 \left[\dfrac{LWG\ (6.28 + 0.0188\ W)}{(1 - 0.3\ LWG)} \right]$ (Table 14)

Animal Production Level: APL = $\dfrac{E_m + E_p}{E_m}$ (Table 12)

Efficiency of ME utilisation for maintenance and production,
$$k_{mp} = \frac{MEF \times APL}{1.39\ MEF + 23\ (APL - 1)}$$

Net Energy for maintenance and production
$$NE_{mp} = \frac{(MEF)^2 \times APL}{1.39\ MEF + 23\ (APL - 1)} \qquad \text{(Table 13)}$$

Section IV—Use of the Metabolisable Energy system for sheep

Pregnant and lactating ewes

Use of the metabolisable energy system for pregnant and lactating sheep is similar to that for dairy cows. Maintenance and production requirements are calculated separately and then summed to give the total requirement.

Metabolisable Energy allowance for maintenance

The minimum requirement for energy for maintenance is equal to the fasting metabolism (FM) which may be calculated as follows:
$$FM(MJ/day) = 0.23 \ W^{0.73}$$
The efficiency of utilisation of metabolisable energy for maintenance (k_m) for sheep has been taken as being constant at 0.70. For rapid calculation a linear relationship between the metabolisable energy requirement and liveweight may be assumed with little error. With the use of the usual 0.05 safety margin, the maintenance allowance for metabolisable energy for ewes kept *indoors* may be calculated as follows:
$$M_m = 1.4 + 0.09 \ W \tag{36}$$
An activity allowance of 0.15 of the fasting metabolism would seem to be justified for ewes living outdoors and the net energy requirement for maintenance is then
$$E_m = 0.265 \ W^{0.73}$$
Using $k_m = 0.70$ and 0.05 safety margin, the equation for calculating maintenance allowance for ewes *outdoors* becomes
$$M_m = 1.8 + 0.1W \tag{37}$$
Maintenance allowances for ewes of various weights are given in Table 15.

Metabolisable Energy allowance for pregnancy

Pregnancy increases total energy requirement, which is needed for two main purposes:
1. To provide the energy stored in the foetus, its associated membranes, and for the growth of uterine tissue, (E_c).
2. To allow for the 'Heat Increment of Gestation' (HIG). This is the additional output of heat that occurs during pregnancy and results from

(a) energy used to synthesise foetal and associated tissues
(b) energy needed to maintain the foetus plus the additional maintenance needs of the ewe resulting from the higher basal metabolism associated with pregnancy.

It is considered that half of the heat increment of gestation (HIG) may be allocated to each of (a) and (b). Hence the energy needs of pregnancy may be calculated as follows:

$$E_c + \frac{HIG}{2} + \frac{HIG}{2 \times k_m}$$

Since k_m is 0.70, the efficiency of ME utilisation for maintenance, this becomes
$$E_c + 1.21 \text{ HIG}$$
Since by definition, ME = net energy + heat production,
extra ME required for pregnancy = $E_c + 1.21$ HIG
Thus the total ME requirement for a pregnant ewe is given by

$$\text{ME required} = M_m + E_c + 1.21 \text{ HIG} \qquad (38)$$

As a basis for calculating the requirements for pregnant sheep, the birthweights of lambs given in Table D have been assumed (Donald and Russell, 1970)[1].

Table D—Lamb birthweights

Ewe weight (kg)	Total lamb weight (kg)	
	Single	Twins
40	3.4	5.4
50	3.9	6.4
60	4.5	7.3
70	5.0	8.2
80	5.5	9.0

Langlands and Sutherland (1968)[2] give estimates of energy stored (E_c) in foetal and associated tissues at various stages during pregnancy for lambs of 4.5 kg birthweight.

Estimates of energy stored by ewes of different weights have been calculated from the data of Langlands and those of Donald and Russell.

Langlands and Sutherland also gave values for the heat increment of gestation (HIG) at various stages of pregnancy for lambs of 4.5 kg birthweights. Estimates for ewes of different weights have been calculated in a similar manner.

By the use of these estimates of E_c and HIG for ewes of different weights, the total daily metabolisable energy allowances for pregnant ewes have been calculated as follows:

$$\text{ME allowance (MJ/day)} = M_m + (E_c + 1.21 \text{ HIG}) \, 1.05$$

which includes the usual 0.05 safety margin on the ME required for pregnancy.

The values obtained are represented accurately by the fitted equations
Ewes with single lambs: $\text{ME} = (1.2 + 0.05 \, W)e^{0.0072t}$ \hfill (39)
Ewes with twin lambs: $\text{ME} = (0.8 + 0.04 \, W)e^{0.0105t}$ \hfill (40)

where t = number of days pregnant
and e = 2.718, the base of the natural logarithm

[1] Anim. Prod. **12**, 273, 1970 [2] Brit. J. Nutr. **22**, 217, 1968

ME allowances for ewes of various bodyweights, (W) carrying either single or twin lambs are shown in Table 15 (page 55).

Formulation of a ration for a pregnant ewe

The following information is needed before proceeding:
(a) liveweight of the ewe, W (kg)
(b) whether the ewe is expected to carry single or twin lambs
(c) number of weeks before lambing
(d) probable dry matter intake, DMI (kg/day)
(e) dry matter content, DM (g/kg), and ME content, MEF (MJ/kg DM), of the foods available.

then calculate:
(f) ME allowance for maintenance and pregnancy
(g) total DM and ME supplied by the foods making up the ration and to compare these with (d) and (f).

Example 19

Formulation of a ration for a 60 kg ewe carrying twin lambs due to lamb in 4 weeks time. The foods available are meadow hay, swedes and sheep compound food.

Probable dry matter appetite = 1.1 kg/day
ME for maintenance and pregnancy = 10.9 MJ/day   (Table 15)

Daily ration		DMI (kg)	ME (MJ)
0.75 kg hay,	(850 g/kg DM, 8 MJ/kg DM)	0.64	5.1
2 kg swedes	(120 g/kg DM, 12.8 MJ/kg DM)	0.24	3.1
0.25 kg compound food	(880 g/kg DM, 12.5 MJ/kg DM)	0.22	2.7
		1.10	10.9

Metabolisable Energy allowances for lactation

The requirement for net energy for milk production is the energy content (E_1) of the milk secreted. This may be obtained from the yield of milk (Y) and its energy value (EV_1).

Energy value of milk: An energy value (EV_1) of 4.6 MJ/kg has been adopted.

Milk yield: The 12-week milk yields (Y) given in table E have been assumed.

Table E Twelve week milk yields of ewes (kg)

Lambs suckled	Hill breeds	Lowland breeds
Single	100	120
Twins	150	170

Milk yield distributions over the first month (Y_1), second month (Y_2) and third month (Y_3) are given by:

Single lamb	Twin lambs
$Y_1 = 0.374\ Y$	$Y_1 = 0.419\ Y$
$Y_2 = 0.361\ Y$	$Y_2 = 0.346\ Y$
$Y_3 = 0.265\ Y$	$Y_3 = 0.235\ Y$

From these ratios, the average expected daily milk yields of lactating ewes have been calculated and are shown in Table 16 (page 55).

Efficiency of utilisation of Metabolisable Energy for milk production
By analogy with the dairy cow, k_1 has been taken as 0.62. The metabolisable energy required to produce a kilogram of milk is then $4.6 \div 0.62 = 7.42$ MJ. Allowing the usual safety margin, this becomes 7.8 MJ. The calculated total ME allowances for hill and lowland ewes with either single or twin lambs are shown in Tables 17 and 18 (page 56).

Formulation of a ration for a lactating ewe
The information needed for this purpose is:
- (a) liveweight of the ewe, W (kg)
- (b) whether it is a hill or lowland ewe
- (c) whether the ewe is suckling single or twin lambs
- (d) stage of lactation
- (e) expected dry matter appetite, DMI (kg/day)
- (f) dry matter content, DM (g/kg) and ME content, MEF (MJ/kg DM), of the foods available

then calculate:
- (g) ME allowance for maintenance, M_m (MJ/day)
- (h) ME allowance for lactation, M_l (MJ/day)
- (i) total ME allowance, $M_m + M_l$ (MJ/day)
- (j) total DM and ME supplied by the foods making up the ration and compare these with (i) and (e)

Example 20
Formulation of a ration for a 40 kg hill ewe suckling a single lamb in the first month of lactation. The foods available are barn dried hay and oats.

Dry matter appetite	=	1.6 kg/day	
ME for maintenance M_m	=	5.8 MJ/day	(Table 15)
Milk yield in 1st month	=	1.34 kg/day	(Table 16)
ME for lactation, M_l	=	1.34 × 7.8 = 10.5 MJ/day	
Total ME required	=	$M_m + M_l$ = 5.8 + 10.5	
		= 16.3 MJ/day	(Table 17)

Daily ration

	DMI (kg)	ME (MJ)
1.2 kg hay, (830 g/kg DM, 9.5 MJ/kg DM)	1.00	9.5
0.7 kg oats, (860 g/kg DM, 11.5 MJ/kg DM)	0.60	6.9
	1.60	16.4

Thus a daily ration of 1.2 kg hay as fed and 0.7 kg oats as fed will meet the energy needs of a 40 kg lactating ewe with a single lamb and does not exceed the limit of her dry matter intake.

Note If two foods only are involved in the ration, use can be made of equation (23) as in earlier sections:

$$FD = \frac{DMI (MC - M/D)}{(MC - MF)} \text{ kg/day} \qquad (23)$$

The required energy concentration M/D for Example 20 is

$$M/D = \frac{ME}{DMI} = \frac{16.3}{1.6} = 10.2 \text{ MJ/kg DM}$$

Table 15—ME allowances (MJ/day) of pregnant ewes outdoors

| Liveweight, W (kg) | Maintenance | Weeks before lambing |||||
		8	6	4	2	Birth
30 S	4.8	5.1	5.7	6.3	6.9	7.7
T	*(− 0.7)	5.1	5.9	6.8	7.9	9.2
40 S	5.8	6.1	6.7	7.4	8.2	9.1
T	*(− 0.8)	6.1	7.1	8.2	9.5	11.0
50 S	6.8	7.0	7.8	8.6	9.5	10.5
T	*(− 0.9)	7.1	8.3	9.6	11.1	12.8
60 S	7.8	8.0	8.8	9.8	10.8	11.9
T	*(− 1.0)	8.1	9.4	10.9	12.7	14.7
70 S	8.8	8.9	9.9	10.9	12.1	13.4
T	*(− 1.1)	9.2	10.6	12.3	14.2	16.5
80 S	9.8	9.9	10.9	12.1	13.4	14.8
T	*(− 1.2)	10.2	11.8	13.7	15.8	18.3

(including safety margin)
*For ewes indoors decrease by allowance shown thus (− 1.2)
Based on $M_m = 1.8 + 0.1 W$ (outdoors), $M_m = 1.4 + 0.09 W$ (indoors)
S = singles: $M_m = (1.2 + 0.05 W)e^{0.0072t}$
T = twins: $M_m = (0.8 + 0.04 W)e^{0.0105t}$
(where t = number of days pregnant)

Table 16—Average daily milk yield, (kg/day) of lactating ewes

| Breed | Lambs | Milk yield (kg/day) |||
		Month 1	Month 2	Month 3
Hill	Single	1.34	1.29	0.95
	Twins	2.24	1.85	1.26
Lowland	Single	1.60	1.55	1.14
	Twins	2.54	2.10	1.43

Table 17—ME allowances (MJ/day) for lactating hill ewes

| Liveweight, W (kg) | Lambs | Stage of lactation |||
		Month 1	Month 2	Month 3
30	Single	15.3	14.9	12.2
	Twins	22.3	19.2	14.6
40	Single	16.3	15.9	13.2
	Twins	23.3	20.2	15.6
50	Single	17.3	16.9	14.2
	Twins	24.3	21.2	16.6
60	Single	18.3	17.9	15.2
	Twins	25.3	22.2	17.6

(including safety margin)

Table 18—ME allowances (MJ/day) for lactating lowland ewes

| Liveweight, W (kg) | Lambs | Stage of lactation |||
		Month 1	Month 2	Month 3
50	Single	19.3	18.9	15.7
	Twins	26.6	23.2	18.0
60	Single	20.3	19.9	16.7
	Twins	27.6	24.2	19.0
70	Single	21.3	20.9	17.7
	Twins	28.6	25.2	20.0
80	Single	22.3	21.9	18.7
	Twins	29.6	26.2	21.0

(including safety margin)

Growing and fattening sheep: use of the Metabolisable Energy system to predict performance

The efficiency of ME utilisation for maintenance, growth and fattening in lambs closely resembles that of growing cattle described in Section III. Equations defining net energy requirements for maintenance and gain will obviously be different, and are detailed below.

Metabolisable Energy allowances for maintenance
For animals kept indoors the net energy required for maintenance (E_m) is equal to the fasting metabolism (FM) and may be calculated from the equation

$$E_m \text{ (MJ/day)} = 0.29 \ W^{0.73} \tag{41}$$

The efficiency with which metabolisable energy is used for maintenance (k_m) is 0.70 and the requirement for metabolisable energy for maintenance is

$$\frac{E_m}{0.70} \text{ or } 1.43 \ E_m$$

With the usual safety margin, the maintenance allowance becomes $0.435 W^{0.73}$. For rapid calculation, a linear relationship between the allowance of metabolisable energy for maintenance and liveweight may be adopted with little loss of accuracy. The equation for calculating maintenance allowance is then

$$M_m = 1.2 + 0.13\ W \tag{42}$$

Table 19—Maintenance allowances for growing sheep

Liveweight, W (kg)	ME allowance (M/J day)	
	Indoors[1]	Outdoors[2]
10	2.5	2.9
15	3.2	3.7
20	3.8	4.4
25	4.5	5.2
30	5.1	5.9
35	5.8	6.7
40	6.4	7.4
45	7.1	8.2
50	7.7	8.9

[1] Based on $M_m = 1.2 + 0.13\ W$
[2] Based on $M_m = 1.4 + 0.15\ W$
} including safety margin

For animals kept outdoors an activity increment of 0.15 of the fasting metabolism should be added and the metabolisable energy allowance for maintenance is then

$$M_m = 0.50\ W^{0.73}$$

For rapid calculation a linear relationship between maintenance allowance and liveweight may be adopted with little loss of accuracy. The equation for calculating maintenance allowance then becomes

$$M_m = 1.4 + 0.15\ W \tag{43}$$

Allowances of ME for maintenance (MJ/day) for growing and fattening sheep, both indoors and outdoors, are given in Table 19.

Where animals are kept under conditions involving additional expenditure of energy, e.g., under adverse climatic conditions or where food is scarce and extra foraging is required, it may be necessary to increase the maintenance allowances above those suggested.

Metabolisable Energy allowances for prediction of liveweight gain

The efficiency with which the metabolisable energy available for production (MEP) is utilised for body gain (k_g) may be calculated as for cattle:

$$k_g = 0.0435\ M/D \tag{8}$$

The energy stored (E_g) is then calculated as the product of metabolisable energy available for production (MEP) and its efficiency of utilisation (k_g), i.e.,

Energy stored as gain E_g = MEP × k_g = MEP × 0.0435 M/D

Including the usual safety margin this becomes

$$E_g = MEP \times 0.0414 \text{ M/D} \tag{27}$$

Values of energy stored for given amounts of metabolisable energy available for production, at various energy concentrations (M/D), are given in Table 20.

The weight gain that can be achieved from the energy stored can be calculated as follows:

$$LWG = \frac{\text{Energy stored}}{\text{Energy value of gain}} = \frac{E_g}{EV_g}$$

Energy value of gain

Details of the energy value of liveweight gain by lambs are given in Nutrient Requirements of Farm Livestock No 2 *Ruminants* ARC 1965, Appendix 6.2, Table 3 p.255. These values are accurately represented by the equation

$$\log_{10} EV_g = 0.11 \log_{10} LWG + 0.004W + 0.88 \text{ (MJ/kg)} \tag{44}$$

where W is kg, and LWG is **g/day**

Predicted liveweight gain

With the substitution of $\frac{E_g}{LWG}$ for EV_g equation (44) may be rearranged to give the following:

$$\log_{10} LWG = 0.9 \log_{10} E_g - 0.0036 W + 1.91 \tag{45}$$

Values for gain predicted from energy stored, (E_g) and bodyweight (W) are given in Table 21.

Table 20—Energy stored E_g, from ME available MEP, at energy concentration M/D

MEP (MJ)	Energy concentration, M/D (MJ/kg DM)						
	8	9	10	11	12	13	14
2	0.7	0.7	0.8	0.9	1.0	1.1	1.2
4	1.3	1.5	1.7	1.8	2.0	2.2	2.3
6	2.0	2.2	2.5	2.7	3.0	3.2	3.5
8	2.6	3.0	3.3	3.6	4.0	4.3	4.6
10	3.3	3.7	4.1	4.6	5.0	5.4	5.8
12	4.0	4.5	5.0	5.5	6.0	6.5	7.0
14	4.6	5.2	5.8	6.4	7.0	7.5	8.1
16	5.3	6.0	6.6	7.3	7.9	8.6	9.3
18	6.0	6.7	7.5	8.2	8.9		
20	6.6	7.5	8.3	9.1			

(including safety margin)
Based on E_g = MEP × 0.0414 M/D

Table 21—Predicted liveweight gain (g/day) from energy stored E_g, for liveweight, W

E_g (MJ)	Liveweight, W(kg)								
	10	15	20	25	30	35	40	45	50
0.5	40	38	37	35	34	33	31	30	29
1.0	75	72	69	66	63	61	58	56	54
1.5	108	103	99	95	91	88	84	81	77
2.0	140	134	129	123	118	114	109	105	100
2.5	171	164	157	151	145	139	133	128	123
3.0	201	193	185	178	170	164	157	151	144
3.5	231	222	213	204	196	188	180	173	166
4.0	261	250	240	230	221	212	203	195	187
4.5	290	278	267	256	245	236	226	217	208
5.0		306	293	282	270	259	249	239	229
5.5			320	307	294	282	271	260	249
6.0			346	332	318	305	293	281	270
6.5				357	342	328	315	302	290
7.0				381	365	351	337	323	310
7.5				406	389	373	358	344	330
8.0					412	396	380	364	349
8.5					435	418	401	386	369
9.0						440	422	405	388

Based on $\log_{10} \text{LWG} = 0.9 \log_{10} E_g - 0.0036W + 1.91$

Prediction of the liveweight gain of growing sheep

This can be done in a similar manner to that for beef cattle.
It is necessary to know the following:
   (a) liveweight of the animal, W (kg)
   (b) total metabolisable energy supplied by the ration, MER (MJ/day)
   (c) dry matter intake of the ration, DMI (kg/day)
and to calculate:
   (d) metabolisable energy concentration of the ration, M/D (MJ/kg DM)
   (e) metabolisable energy required for maintenance, M_m (MJ/day)
   (f) metabolisable energy available for production, MEP (MJ/day)
   (g) net energy available for production, E_g (MJ/day)
   (h) predicted liveweight gain, LWG (g/day)

The following examples illustrate the method of calculation.

Example 21
Prediction of the liveweight gain of a lamb weighing 40 kg kept indoors, receiving the following ration:

		DMI (kg)	ME (MJ)
0.75 kg hay,	(830 g/kg DM, 8 MJ/kg DM)	0.62	5.0
0.70 kg compound food,	(880 g/kg DM, 12 MJ/kg DM)	0.62	7.4
		1.24	12.4

Ration energy concentration M/D = $\frac{12.4}{1.24}$ = 10 MJ/kg DM

Maintenance ME, M_m = 6.4 MJ (Table 19)

The metabolisable energy available for production can be found by deducting that required for maintenance from the total metabolisable energy of the ration.

ME available for liveweight gain, MEP = MER — M_m = 12.4 — 6.4
= 6 MJ

Energy stored as gain, E_g = MEP × 0.0414 × M/D
= 6 × 0.0414 × 10
= 2.5 MJ/day (Table 20)

Predicted liveweight gain LWG = 133 g/day (Table 21)

Example 22
Prediction of liveweight gain of a 25 kg lamb kept outdoors, receiving a ration consisting of:

		DMI (kg)	ME (MJ)
2.5 kg silage,	(200 g/kg DM, 9.5 MJ/kg DM)	0.50	4.8
1.0 kg swedes,	(110 g/kg DM, 12.8 MJ/kg DM)	0.11	1.4
0.3 kg compound food,	(860 g/kg DM, 12.5 MJ/kg DM)	0.26	3.2
		0.87	9.4

MER = 9.4 MJ/day
M/D = $\frac{9.4}{0.87}$ = 10.8 MJ/kg DM
M_m = 5.2 MJ (Table 19)
MEP = 9.4 — 5.2 = 4.2 MJ/day
E_g = 4.2 × 0.0414 × 10.8 = 1.9 MJ/day (Table 20)
LWG = 116 g/day (Table 21)

Metabolisable Energy allowances for growing and fattening lambs
The total ME allowances for growing lambs can be calculated by summing the allowance for maintenance (M_m) given by equations (42) and (43) and the ME for production (M_g) which is given by

$$M_g = \frac{E_g}{0.0414 \, M/D} \quad (27a)$$

Estimates of the total ME allowances for lambs of different weights, gaining at different daily rates, on rations of different energy concentration (M/D), are given in Table 22. An increase in maintenance of 0.15 for *outdoor* fed sheep is also shown in Table 22 (page 63).

Growing and fattening sheep: use of a variable Net Energy system

This system states the allowances for the animal in terms of net energy. Net energies are calculated for each food, at the relevant level of animal production, and used, in conjunction with the estimates of requirements, to formulate rations. The system is additive and ideal for linear programme work. Replacement values can be calculated without the iterative approach necessary with the metabolisable energy system.

Table 22—Daily ME allowances (MJ/day) for indoor fed growing sheep

Liveweight (kg)	Ration M/D (MJ/kg DM)	Rate of gain (g/day)							
		50	100	150	200	250	300	350	400
10 (+ 0.4)*	8	4.4							
	10	4.0	5.8						
	12	3.8	5.3	6.9					
	14	3.6	4.9	6.2					
15 (+ 0.5)*	8	5.2	7.5						
	10	4.8	6.6	8.6					
	12	4.5	6.1	7.7	9.4				
	14	4.3	5.6	7.1	8.5				
20 (+ 0.6)*	8	5.9	8.4	11.0					
	10	5.5	7.5	9.5	11.7				
	12	5.2	6.8	8.6	10.4	12.2	14.1		
	14	5.0	6.4	7.9	9.4	11.0	12.6		
25 (+ 0.7)*	8	6.7	9.2	12.0					
	10	6.2	8.3	10.5	12.7	15.0			
	12	5.9	7.6	9.5	11.3	13.3	15.3	17.3	
	14	5.7	7.2	8.7	10.4	12.0	13.7	15.4	
30 (+0.8)*	8	7.4	10.1	13.0					
	10	7.0	9.1	11.4	13.8	16.2			
	12	6.6	8.4	10.3	12.3	14.3	16.4	18.5	
	14	6.4	8.0	9.6	11.3	13.0	14.8	16.6	
35 (+ 0.9)*	8	8.2	11.0	14.0	17.1				
	10	7.7	9.9	12.3	14.8	17.4	20.0		
	12	7.4	9.2	11.2	13.3	15.4	17.6	19.8	22.1
	14	7.1	8.7	10.5	12.2	14.0	15.9	17.8	19.7
40 (+ 1.0)*	8	8.9	11.9	15.0	18.3				
	10	8.4	10.8	13.3	15.9	18.6	21.3		
	12	8.1	10.1	12.1	14.3	16.5	18.8	21.1	23.5
	14	7.9	9.5	11.3	13.2	15.1	17.0	19.0	21.0
45 (+ 1.1)*	8	9.7	12.8	16.1	19.5				
	10	9.2	11.7	14.3	17.0	19.8	22.6		
	12	8.8	10.9	13.1	15.3	17.7	20.0	22.5	24.9
	14	8.6	10.3	12.2	14.1	16.1	18.2	20.2	22.4
50 (+ 1.2)*	8	10.5	13.7	17.2	20.7				
	10	9.9	12.5	15.3	18.1	21.0	24.0		
	12	9.6	11.7	14.0	16.4	18.8	21.3	23.8	26.4
	14	9.3	11.1	13.1	15.1	17.2	19.4	21.5	23.7

(including safety margin)
*Outdoor fed growing sheep, increase in maintenance allowance of 0.15 indicated as MJ/head daily thus (+0.8)

Net Energy allowance for maintenance

Animals kept indoors The net energy allowance for maintenance (E_m) may be calculated from equation (41),

$$E_m \text{ (MJ/day)} = 0.29 \, W^{0.73} \tag{41}$$

If a safety margin of 0.05 is used the daily net energy allowance for maintenance becomes

$$E_m \text{ (MJ/day)} = 0.3045 \, W^{0.73}$$

For rapid calculation a linear relationship between liveweight and net energy allowance for maintenance may be assumed with little loss of accuracy. The equation for calculating maintenance allowance is then

$$E_m \text{ (MJ/day)} = 0.84 + 0.091 \, W \tag{46}$$

Animals kept outdoors For such animals an activity increment of 0.15 of the fasting metabolism may be added and the net energy allowance for maintenance, (E_m) may be calculated by the following equation:

$$E_m \text{ (MJ/day)} = 0.3502 \, W^{0.73}$$

For rapid calculation a linear relationship between weight and daily net energy allowance for maintenance may be assumed. The equation for calculating maintenance allowance is then

$$E_m \text{ (MJ/day)} = 1.1 + 0.1 \, W \tag{47}$$

Net Energy allowance for liveweight gain

The net energy required for production (E_p) is the energy stored in liveweight gain, which is the product of the gain (LWG) and its energy value (EV_g). The energy stored as gain in sheep (E_p) may be calculated from the following equation:

$$\log_{10} E_p = 1.11 \log_{10} LWG + 0.004 \, W - 2.10 \tag{48}$$

where LWG is g/day and a safety margin is included.

The maintenance allowance may be combined with the estimate of production to give the total daily net energy allowance shown in Table 23.

Animal Production Level

In the metabolisable energy system for lambs, the efficiency of utilisation of metabolisable energy for maintenance is fixed at 0.70 while the efficiency for growth is dependent upon the dietary metabolisable energy concentration:

$$k_g = 0.0435 \, M/D \tag{8}$$

The overall efficiency of utilisation of metabolisable energy for maintenance and growth (k_{mp}) depends upon the proportions of the energy used for the two functions and upon the dietary metabolisable energy concentration (M/D). At any given value of M/D and level of production, defined relative to maintenance, k_{mp} will be constant.

The level of production relative to maintenance is referred to as the Animal Production Level and is defined as the ratio between maintenance and production requirements in terms of their net energies. APL may be calculated as follows:

$$APL = \frac{E_m + E_p}{E_m} \tag{19}$$

exactly as defined in Section III on beef cattle. In this case however E_m is defined by equations (46) or (47) and E_p by equation (48).

Animals kept indoors Values for APL at different liveweights and daily weight gains for sheep kept indoors are shown in Table 24. At the maintenance level, when gain is zero, $APL = 1.0$

Animals kept outdoors Owing to the inclusion of an activity increment for animals kept outdoors, values of APL will be slightly lower than for comparable animals kept indoors. The effect on the net energy values of food is negligible (*circa* 0.1 MJ/kg) and the values given in Table 25 can be used for indoor and outdoor conditions.

Net Energy for maintenance and production

The overall efficiency of utilisation of ME for maintenance and production (k_{mp}) is variable, depending on the proportions of ME used for maintenance and fattening. It may be defined as the ratio of net energy requirement for maintenance and production, to the total metabolisable energy requirement (M_{mp}):

$$k_{mp} = \frac{E_m + E_p}{M_{mp}} \tag{18}$$

and $M_{mp} = M_m + M_p$

Hence $$k_{mp} = \frac{E_m + E_p}{M_m + M_p} \tag{32}$$

Using the general expression $ME = \frac{NE}{k}$,

$$M_m = \frac{E_m}{0.70}$$

$$M_p = \frac{E_p}{0.0435 \quad M/D}$$

Since $APL = \frac{E_m + E_p}{E_m}$, then $E_p = E_m (APL - 1)$

and $$M_p = \frac{E_m (APL - 1)}{0.0435 \quad M/D}$$

Substituting in equation (32) and rearranging:

$$k_{mp} = \frac{E_m + E_p}{M_m + M_p}$$

$$k_{mp} = \frac{M/D \times APL}{1.43 \, M/D + 23 \, (APL - 1)} \tag{49}$$

Table 23—Net Energy allowances (MJ) for growing lambs (indoors)

LWG (g/day)	Liveweight, W (kg)								
	10	15	20	25	30	35	40	45	50
50	2.4	2.9	3.4	3.9	4.4	4.9	5.4	5.9	6.4
100	3.2	3.7	4.2	4.8	5.3	5.8	6.4	6.9	7.5
150	4.0	4.6	5.2	5.7	6.3	6.9	7.5	8.1	8.7
200	4.9	5.5	6.1	6.7	7.3	8.0	8.6	9.3	9.9
250	5.8	6.4	7.1	7.7	8.4	9.1	9.8	10.5	11.2
300		7.3	8.0	8.8	9.5	10.2	11.0	11.7	12.5
350			9.0	9.8	10.6	11.4	12.2	13.0	13.8
400				10.9	11.7	12.5	13.4	14.3	15.2
Outdoors	+0.3	+0.4	+0.4	+0.5	+0.5	+0.6	+0.6	+0.7	+0.7

(including safety margin)
Based on NE allowance = $E_m + E_p$ (equations 47 and 48)
Requirements for lambs *outdoors* should be increased by amounts shown in final row at base of table.

Table 24—Animal Production Levels (APL) for growing sheep

LWG (g/day)	Liveweight, W (kg)								
	10	15	20	25	30	35	40	45	50
50	1.38	1.32	1.28	1.25	1.23	1.21	1.20	1.19	1.18
100	1.83	1.69	1.60	1.53	1.49	1.45	1.43	1.41	1.39
150	2.30	2.08	1.94	1.84	1.77	1.71	1.67	1.64	1.61
200	2.79	2.49	2.29	2.15	2.05	1.98	1.92	1.88	1.84
250	3.29	2.90	2.65	2.48	2.35	2.25	2.18	2.12	2.08
300		3.33	3.02	2.81	2.65	2.54	2.44	2.37	2.32
350			3.40	3.15	2.96	2.82	2.71	2.63	2.56
400				3.49	3.27	3.11	2.99	2.89	2.81

Based on APL = $\dfrac{E_m + E_p}{E_m}$

Net Energy values of foods for maintenance and production

The k_{mp} values may be used to calculate net energies for maintenance and production (NE_{mp}) for either foods or rations as follows:

$$NE_{mp} = MEF \times k_{mp}$$

$$= \frac{(MEF)^2 \times APL}{1.43\ MEF + 23\ (APL - 1)} \qquad (50)$$

Values for NE_{mp} for different values of APL and MEF are given in Table 25.

Table 25—Net Energies of foods for maintenance and production, NE$_{mp}$(MJ/kg DM)

APL	Metabolisable energy of food, MEF (MJ/kg DM)								
	6	7	8	9	10	11	12	13	14
1.0	4.2	4.9	5.6	6.3	7.0	7.7	8.4	9.1	9.8
1.1	3.6	4.4	5.1	5.9	6.6	7.4	8.1	8.9	9.7
1.2	3.3	4.0	4.8	5.6	6.3	7.1	7.9	8.7	9.6
1.3	3.0	3.8	4.5	5.3	6.1	7.0	7.8	8.6	9.5
1.4	2.8	3.6	4.3	5.1	6.0	6.8	7.6	8.5	9.4
1.5	2.7	3.4	4.2	5.0	5.8	6.7	7.5	8.4	9.3
1.6	2.6	3.3	4.1	4.9	5.7	6.6	7.4	8.3	9.3
1.7	2.5	3.2	4.0	4.8	5.6	6.5	7.4	8.3	9.2
1.8	2.4	3.1	3.9	4.7	5.5	6.4	7.3	8.2	9.2
1.9	2.3	3.0	3.8	4.6	5.4	6.3	7.2	8.2	9.1
2.0	2.3	3.0	3.7	4.5	5.4	6.2	7.2	8.1	9.1
2.2	2.2	2.9	3.6	4.4	5.3	6.1	7.1	8.0	9.1
2.4	2.1	2.8	3.5	4.3	5.2	6.1	7.0	8.0	9.0
2.6	2.1	2.7	3.4	4.2	5.1	6.0	6.9	7.9	9.0
2.8	2.0	2.7	3.4	4.2	5.0	5.9	6.9	7.9	8.9
3.0	2.0	2.6	3.3	4.1	5.0	5.9	6.8	7.8	8.9

Based on $NE_{mp} = \dfrac{(MEF)^2 \times APL}{1.43\ MEF + 23\ (APL - 1)}$

Use of the variable Net Energy system for ration formulation

Within dry matter appetite limits, rations for growing sheep can be constructed in a simple additive manner by using the appropriate NE$_{mp}$ values for the desired animal production level. In order to do this, it is necessary to know the following:

(a) animal's liveweight, W (kg)
(b) required rate of liveweight gain, LWG (g/day)
(c) expected dry matter intake, DMI (kg/day)
(d) food dry matter content, DM (g/kg)
and ME content, MEF (MJ/kg DM)

and to calculate:

(e) required animal production level, APL
(f) net energy allowance for maintenance and gain (MJ/day)
(g) appropriate NE$_{mp}$ values for each food (MJ/kg DM)
and to formulate a ration which meets the values in (f) and (c)

Example 23

Formulation of a ration for a 35 kg lamb to gain 100 g/day
Foods available, hay, MEF 8 MJ/kg DM
cereal, MEF 13 MJ/kg DM
Dry matter intake, DMI = 1.0 kg/day
Net energy required for maintenance, E$_m$ = 4.0 MJ/day
gain, E$_g$ = 1.8 MJ/day
5.8 MJ/day   (Table 23)

Animal production level = $\dfrac{E_m}{E_g}$ = $\dfrac{5.8}{4.0}$ = 1.45 (Table 24)

NE$_{mp}$ of hay,   MEF 8 MJ/kg DM   = 4.2 MJ/kg DM   (Table 25)
NE$_{mp}$ of cereal, MEF 13 ME/kg DM   = 8.4 MJ/kg DM

Daily ration

	DMI (kg)	NE (MJ)
0.6 kg hay DM at 4.2 MJ/kg DM	0.60	2.5
0.4 kg cereal DM at 8.4 MJ/kg DM	0.40	3.4
	1.00	5.9

If both hay and cereal have dry matter contents of 850 g/kg a daily ration of 0.71 kg hay and 0.47 kg cereal will produce the required rate of gain within the constraint of dry matter intake.

Calculation of replacement values of foods

Example 24
Calculation of the replacement value of hay, (8 MJ/kg DM) for maize (14 MJ/kg DM) when fed to:
(a) a 25 kg lamb growing at 200 g/day
(b) a 35 kg lamb growing at 150 g/day

(a)   Animal production level = 2.15   (Table 24)
       Hay, NE$_{mp}$ = 3.6 MJ/kg DM
       Maize NE$_{mp}$ = 9.1 MJ/kg DM   (Table 25)
       Replacement value of hay for maize = $\dfrac{9.1}{3.6}$ = 2.53

(b)   APL = 1.71
       Hay NE$_{mp}$ = 4.0
       Maize NE$_{mp}$ = 9.2
       Replacement value = $\dfrac{9.2}{4.0}$ = 2.30

Summary

ME system for pregnant ewes

Maintenance allowance: $M_m = 1.8 + 0.1\,W$ (outdoors)
(including safety margin) $M_m = 1.4 + 0.09\,W$ (indoors)   } (Table 15)

ME allowance for maintenance and pregnancy
Ewes with single lambs: $M_{mp} = (1.2 + 0.05\,W)e^{0.0072t}$ (Table 15)
(including safety margin)
Ewes with twin lambs: $M_{mp} = (0.8 + 0.04\,W)e^{0.0105t}$ (Table 15)
(including safety margin)
where t = number of days pregnant

ME system for lactating ewes
Maintenance allowance $M_m = 1.8 + 0.1\ W$ (outdoors)
(including safety margin) $M_m = 1.4 + 0.09\ W$ (indoors)   (Table 15)

Production allowances
Energy value of milk: $EV_l = 4.6$ MJ/kg
Energy secreted as milk: $E_l = 4.6\ Y$ MJ/day
Efficiency of ME utilisation
   for lactation $k_l = 0.62$
ME allowance for milk: $M_l = 7.8\ Y$ MJ/kg
(including safety margin)

ME system for growing sheep
Maintenance allowance $M_m = 1.2 + 0.13\ W$ (indoors)
(including safety margin) $M_m = 1.4 + 0.15\ W$ (outdoors)   (Table 19)

Production allowances
ME available for liveweight gain: $MEP = MER - M_m$
Efficiency of utilisation of ME for gain: $k_g = 0.0435\ M/D$
Energy stored as gain: $E_g = MEP \times k_g = MEP \times 0.0414\ M/D$ (Table 20)
                            (including safety margin)

Energy value of gain: $\log_{10} EV_g = 0.11 \log_{10} LWG + 0.004\ W + 0.88$ (MJ/kg)

Predicted liveweight gain: $\log_{10} LWG = 0.9 \log_{10} E_g - 0.0036\ W + 1.91$
   where LWG is g/day   (Table 21)

Variable Net Energy system for growing sheep
Net energy for maintenance
(including safety margin) $E_m = 0.84 + 0.091\ W$ MJ/day (indoors)
                                  $E_m = 1.10 + 0.1\ W$ MJ/day (outdoors)

Net Energy for liveweight gain
(including safety margin)
$\log_{10} E_p = 1.11 \log_{10} LWG + 0.004\ W - 2.10$ MJ/day   (Table 23)
Animal Production Level: $APL = \dfrac{E_m + E_p}{E_m}$ (Table 24)
Efficiency of ME utilisation for maintenance and production
$$k_{mp} = \frac{M/D \times APL}{1.43\ M/D + 23\ (APL - 1)}$$

Net Energy for maintenance and production
$$NE_{mp} = \frac{(MEF)^2 \times APL}{1.43\ MEF + 23\ (APL - 1)}\ \text{MJ/kg DM} \quad \text{(Table 25)}$$

Section V—Calculation of the Metabolisable Energies of foods

Energy values of foods

The starting point for the measurement or calculation of the metabolisable energy (ME) of a food is its gross energy or energy value (EV). This can be measured in a bomb calorimeter as MJ/kg dry matter, or calculated from a knowledge of its chemical composition by use of the following equation:

EV (MJ/kg DM) = 0.0226 CP + 0.0407 EE + 0.0192 CF + 0.0177 NFE

where CP is crude protein (N × 6.25)   (51)
EE is ether extract   *all as g/kg DM*
CF is crude fibre   (= 10 × % in DM)
NFE is nitrogen free extractives

This equation was published by workers at the Oskar Kellner Institute, GDR, and has a low residual standard deviation (±0.2 MJ/kg DM). Values for gross energy in the tables of food composition, which follow, have been calculated from this equation.

The higher coefficients for ether extract (oils and fats) and also crude protein result in higher energy values for feeds containing large amounts of these two components. The majority of foods given to cattle and sheep are low in ether extract and the mean energy value calculated from equation (51) is 18.1 MJ/kg DM. Oil seeds, legumes, oil cakes and meals, and animal by-products which may be high in oil and/or protein have values of 20 to 26 MJ/kg DM.

Measured gross energies of foods have in the past been taken to average 4.4 kcal/g DM, equivalent to 18.4 MJ/kg DM. Measurements on grass hay agree exactly with this value, but recent measurements on grass silage averaged 20 MJ/kg DM when volatile compounds were included.

Digestibility measurements on foods

The results of *in vivo* digestibility trials are available in publications such as Morrison's *Feeds and Feeding*, Schneider's *Feeds of the World*, formerly in MAFF Bulletin 48 *Rations for Livestock*, and latterly in ADAS Booklet 2087 *Nutrient allowances and composition of feedingstuffs for ruminants*. Values are given for digestible nutrients as percentages; alternatively the digestibility coefficients of the nutrients are quoted alongside the chemical composition of the food, as in the tables which follow at the end of this section.

Digestible crude protein (DCP, g/kg DM) values are quoted in the tables because they are normally required for ration calculations.

Other methods of expressing digestibility are:

$$\% \text{ Digestibility of the dry matter (DMD)} = \frac{(\text{Food DM} - \text{Faeces DM})}{\text{Food DM}} \times 100 \quad (52)$$

$$\% \text{ Digestibility of the organic matter (OMD)} = \frac{(\text{Food OM} - \text{Faeces OM})}{\text{Food OM}} \times 100 \quad (53)$$

$$\% \text{ Digestible organic matter in dry matter (DOMD)} = \frac{(\text{Food OM} - \text{Faeces OM})}{\text{Food DM}} \times 100 \quad (54)$$

Care must be exercised in using or comparing results to ensure that the relevant unit is being used.

Equation (52) for DMD avoids the need for total ash measurements of the food and residue, but introduces a source of error since ash has no energy value and can be very variable.

Equation (53) for OMD is often used for research purposes since it eliminates ash variation from comparisons of digestibilities. However OMD values can be applied only to food intake expressed as organic matter and this is rarely done.

It follows that OMD values can be converted to DOMD values if the ash content of the food is known:

$$\text{DOMD \%} = \frac{\text{OMD \% } (100 - \text{Ash \%})}{100} \quad (55)$$

The most useful method of expression for food evaluation purposes is DOMD, which enables the calculation of ME as MJ/kg DM directly. In the tables which follow *in vivo* DOMD (D values) have been calculated by summing the digestible nutrients, but have been stated as percentages and not as g/kg DM so as to give a link with previous methods of expressing food values.

Digestible energy values of foods

Direct measurements of the digestible energy (DE) of foods are fairly widely recorded since it only requires the measurement of the energy value of the food and associated faeces from an *in vivo* digestibility trial.

DE values can be calculated from DOMD by assuming a constant energy value of digested organic matter (e.g. 18.7 MJ/kg DM for dried grass), or by calculating the energy value from a prediction equation. An example of this is one proposed by Osbourn *et al* at the Grassland Research Institute for grass and fresh maize:

$$\text{EV of DOM} = 0.0124 \text{ CP} + 17.3 \text{ (MJ/kg DM)} \quad (56)$$
$$\text{where CP is g/kg DM}$$

In general the following equation can be used for the calculation of digestible energy values:
$$DE = 0.19 \text{ DOMD \%} \quad (MJ/kg \text{ DM}) \tag{57}$$

Metabolisable Energy values of foods

The metabolisable energy of a food (MEF) is defined as
$$MEF = DE - (\text{methane energy} + \text{urine energy})$$
As indicated in Section I, the sum of methane and urine energy is reasonably constant as a proportion of digested energy, averaging 0.19.
$$\text{Thus, ME} = 0.81 \text{ DE} \tag{1}$$
The use of an average value for the energy value of digested organic matter of 19 MJ/kg DM gives the following general equation:
$$MEF = 0.15 \text{ DOMD \% MJ/kg DM} \tag{58}$$
The simple linear relationship is demonstrated in Table F.

Table F—ME values of foods derived from DOMD % values

DOMD %	MEF, (MJ/kg DM)
40	6.00
45	6.75
50	7.50
55	8.25
60	9.00
65	9.75
70	10.50
75	11.25
80	12.00
85	12.75

The ME values listed in the standard tables have been calculated from details of digestible proximate constituents given in ADAS Booklet 2087 by the use of the conversion factors proposed by the Oskar Kellner Institute, Rostock viz.
ME (MJ/kg DM)
$$= 0.0152 \text{ DCP} + 0.0342 \text{ DEE} + 0.0128 \text{ DCF} + 0.0159 \text{ DNFE} \tag{2}$$
where DCP   is digestible crude protein
         DEE   is digestible ether extract   *all as g/kg DM*
         DCF   is digestible crude fibre   (= 10 × % in DM)
         DNFE is digestible nitrogen free extract

The use of this equation was demonstrated in Section I. It has a residual standard deviation of ± 0.3 MJ/kg DM.

The Tables of Food Composition which follow result essentially from a recalculation of existing digestibility data. Revision of these tables must await the accumulation of new data from food evaluation units set up for this purpose.

Revised values for some foods are given on page 74.

The values listed fall into three categories:
1. Values for foods such as barley, maize and soya bean meal that vary little in ME value. The figures quoted are sound averages that are applicable generally. This applies to most well-defined foods in Sections 12, 13 and 14 of the Food Composition Tables.
2. Values for less common foods which are representative examples but which may not have general application, e.g. Sections 7 and 15.
3. Values for forages like hay, silage etc that vary considerably in ME value. The figures quoted are examples only of ME values that may be found for groups of foods of this type.

This last group requires special attention because forages may supply over half of the dry matter of a ration. Consequently variations in ME values influence both ME intake and the M/D value of the diet considerably. More accurate knowledge of the ME of forages available for an individual feeding situation is desirable.

Prediction of the Metabolisable Energy values of forages

ME values of forages may be predicted from chemical analysis or by using *in vitro* digestibility to provide figures from which ME values may be calculated using appropriate regression equations.

The equations available are of 3 types:
1. Those that derive ME from measured DE values for a food:
$$ME_F = 0.81 \, DE \tag{1}$$
2. Those that predict ME from digestibility values, DOMD %:
$$ME_F = 0.15 \, DOMD \, \% \tag{58}$$
where DOMD % can be *in vivo* or calculated from *in vitro* laboratory results.

Reference was made earlier to the three units currently in use to measure digestibility. They are highly correlated when measured *in vitro* on typical forages. The following equations have been derived from statistical study of 134 sets of results from the Tilley and Terry method:
$$DOMD \, \% = 0.98 \, DMD \, \% - 4.8 \tag{59}$$
$$DOMD \, \% = 0.92 \, OMD \, \% - 1.2 \tag{60}$$

Equation (58) can be used on most *in vitro* DOMD values (IVD) of ruminant foods with the exception of high oil or fat containing foods and perhaps very high protein foods.

Where only OMD or DMD values are available, these should first be converted to DOMD values by the use of equations (55), (59) or (60).

Greater precision can be obtained by varying the coefficient according to the class of food as follows:

0.14 for straw.

0.155 for hay, dried grass.

0.16 for roots, leaves of roots, other green foods, grasses, legumes, miscellaneous, cereals and by-products.

3. Those that predict ME values from the chemical composition of the food.

Examples of equations which may be used to predict the ME values of forages are given below. These are subject to periodic review in the light of continuing development work. They are based on analyses for crude fibre (CF), acid detergent fibre (ADF) or modified acid detergent fibre (MADF), and crude protein (CP) sometimes combined with the fibre. It is essential that the correct fibre fraction is used in each equation. Alternatively *in vitro* DOMD content (IVD) may be used.

In these equations, all analyses are expressed as g/kg DM, except for IVD which is kept as a percentage.

Fresh herbage

Grasses

General equations MEF = 15.3 — 0.0153 MADF (61)
MEF = 0.165 IVD — 0.31 (62)

Legumes

MEF = 12.3 — 0.012 MADF (63)

Workers at the Grassland Research Institute have proposed the following equation for grasses, clovers, legumes and maize:

MEF = 0.130 IVD + 0.01 CP + 1.09 (64)

Grass hays

MEF = 16.53 — 0.0213 MADF (65)
MEF = 0.185 IVD — 1.88 (66)

Dried grass and legumes

Dried grass is available in several forms depending on the type of drying plant. The physical form may be long, short chopped, wafered, pelleted or finely ground meal. Drying temperatures may be low (up to 250°C) or high (500-1 000°C).

Low temperature dried grass is usually in long or chopped form and ME values can be predicted from equations (61) to (63) given under 'Fresh herbage'.

Dried grass which has been wafered, ground and/or pelleted has to be treated separately. These processes reduce both the digestibility and metabolisable energy content (calculated as 0.81 × DE) of foods. The effect has been shown on average to be equivalent to an 8 per cent depression of the ME value. However, the efficiency of utilisation of ME is increased to the extent that the net energy of ground pelleted dried grass is approximately equal to that of the original material from which it was prepared. For this class of food, therefore, ME values calculated from digestibility data as 0.18 × DE should be increased by a factor of 1.018 *and no allowance made for increased efficiency of utilisation in subsequent calculations.*

Equations derived from a study of 36 dried grass samples are as follows:

MEF = 15.0 — 0.0166 MADF (67)
MEF = 0.143 IVD + 1.0 (68)

Similar studies on 50 samples of dried lucerne resulted in the following equations:

$$\text{MEF} = 14.7 - 0.0167 \text{ MADF} \tag{69}$$
$$\text{MEF} = 0.163 \text{ IVD} - 0.23 \tag{70}$$

Grass silages

The chemistry of the ensilage process is complex and results in the formation of volatile compounds which are lost on oven drying. Some of these have a high energy value. The contribution these volatile components make to both dry matter content and ME value are very difficult to measure. As a consequence the MEF values of silage, for the time being, continue to be expressed on an oven dry matter basis, using the following equations based on ME = DOMD × 0.16 with no allowance being made for the energy value of volatile components:

General equations

$$\text{MEF} = 14.6 - 0.013 \text{ MADF} \tag{71}$$
$$\text{MEF} = 0.11 \text{ IVD} + 3.2 \tag{72}$$

Maize silage

In vivo studies of 16 samples of maize silage by the Rowett Research Institute Feed Evaluation Unit did not result in any worthwhile prediction equations. A mean value of 11.1 MJ/kg *true* dry matter with a standard deviation of ± 0.6 MJ was recorded. If *in vitro* DOMD values are available, equation (58) may be used to give realistic values.

Estimation of the Metabolisable Energy values of compound foods

With compound foods, the only information normally available under The Feeding Stuffs Regulations 1982 is the declared content of protein (CP), oil (EE), fibre (CF) and ash (TA). Recent work at the Rowett Research Institute Feedingstuffs Evaluation Unit on 24 compound foods resulted in the following equation derived from equation F in Report Number 3 of that Unit:

$$\text{MEF} = 12.0 + 0.008 \text{ CP} + 0.023 \text{ EE} - 0.018 \text{ CF} - 0.012 \text{TA} \tag{73}$$

where all analytical values are expressed as g/kg DM.

Taking inter-laboratory error into account, the standard deviation of the predicted MEF was estimated to be ±0.5 MJ/kg DM.

Equation (2) may be used if the digestibilities of all the nutrients are known. When this information is not available, an *in vitro* estimation of OMD can give an overall mean value for the digestibility of the nutrients. The following equation may then be derived:

$$\text{MEF} = \left[\frac{\text{DOMD}\%}{100 - \text{TA}}\right](0.0152\text{CP} + 0.0342\text{EE} + 0.0128\text{CF} + 0.0159\,\text{NFE}) \tag{74}$$

where all values within the brackets are expressed as g/kg DM. This equation was shown to underestimate MEF by 0.1 MJ/kg DM and to have a standard deviation of ±0.5 MJ/kg DM.

As with forages, equations for predicting the ME values of compound foods are reviewed from time to time.

Revised nutritive values of foods (1983)

		Revised values				Old values			
Food number	Food name	DM g/kg	DOMD %	ME MJ/kg DM	DCP g/kg DM	DM g/kg	DOMD %	ME MJ/kg DM	DCP g/kg DM
105/107	Mangels	100	79	12.4	80	120	79	12.4	80
109	Potatoes	205	88	13.3	80	210	79	12.5	47
110	Sugar beet	200	87	13.7	35	230	87	13.7	35
111	Swede	105	88	13.9	64	120	82	12.8	91
112	Turnip	100	82	12.7	70	90	72	11.2	73
	Fodder beet	180	80	12.5	50	—	—	—	—
207	Turnip leaves	100	70	10.9	130	120	58	9.2	130
304	Kale	130	77	12.1	122	160	71	11.1	106
1201	Barley grain	860	84	12.9	82	860	86	13.7	82
1203	Maize grain	860	88	13.8	69	860	87	14.2	78
1205	Oat grain	860	70	12.0	84	860	68	11.5	84
1208	Wheat grain	860	87	13.5	105	860	87	14.0	105
1501	Apple pomace, fresh	230	57	8.0	30	250	51	8.4	28
1504*	Brewers' grains	280	62	10.4	154	220	59	10.0	149
—	Cassava	880	86	12.8	18	900	80	12.6	20
1528	Maize gluten feed	900	75	12.5	195	900	83	13.5	223
1529	Maize gluten meal	900	92	17.2	736	900	85	14.2	339
1550	Sugar beet pulp, pressed	180	78	12.3	60	180	84	12.7	66
1552	Dried molassed sugar beet pulp	860	82	12.5	80	900	79	12.2	61

*The old data on brewers' grains are expressed on an oven dry matter basis; the revised data are expressed on a corrected dry matter basis to allow for volatile components.

The revised values shown in this table have been compiled from the results of authenticated digestibility trials and chemical analyses carried out since 1970. They were approved in 1983 by the Standing Committee on Tables of Feed Composition. These values do not correspond with the analytical data and digestibility coefficients given in the Tables of Food Composition on pages 75-85, where foods with revised nutritive values are marked with an asterisk*.

Tables of food composition

1 Roots
2 Leaves of roots
3 Other green foods
4 Cereals
5 Grasses
6 Green legumes
7 Miscellaneous
8a Silage—clamp
8b Silage—tower
9 Hay
10 Dried grasses and legumes
11 Straws and chaff
12a Grains and seeds—cereals
12b Legumes
12c Oil seeds
12d Miscellaneous seeds
13 Oil cakes and meals
14 Feedingstuffs of animal origin
15 By-products

Note — Each food marked with an asterisk* in these tables also appears in the table of revised nutritive values of foods given on page 74. When calculating diets for ruminants it is recommended that the revised nutritive values are used, although these do not correspond with the other data set out in the following tables.

Food number	Food name	Dry Matter Content g/kg	Metabolisable Energy MJ/kg DM	Digestible Crude Protein g/kg DM	Crude Protein	Ether Extract	Crude Fibre	N free Extract	Total Ash	Gross Energy MJ/kg DM	Q [ME/GE]	Digestible Organic Matter in Dry Matter DOMD%	Crude Protein	Ether Extract	Crude Fibre	N free Extract	Food number
	1 Roots																
101	Artichoke, Jerusalem	200	13·2	50	75	10	35	825	55	17·4	0·76	84	0·67	0·00	0·29	0·94	101
102	Carrots	130	12·8	62	92	15	108	715	69	17·4	0·73	81	0·67	0·50	0·50	0·96	102
103	Kohlrabi	130	10·8	54	154	8	108	654	77	17·4	0·62	69	0·35	0·00	0·43	0·90	103
104	Mangels, white-fleshed globe	110	12·5	64	91	9	64	773	64	17·3	0·72	79	0·70	0·00	0·43	0·91	104
*105	Mangels, intermediate	120	12·4	58	83	8	58	783	67	17·2	0·72	79	0·70	0·00	0·43	0·90	105
*106	Mangels, yellow-fleshed globe	130	12·4	54	92	8	62	769	69	17·2	0·72	78	0·58	0·00	0·38	0·92	106
107	Mangels, long red	130	12·6	54	77	8	62	785	69	17·1	0·74	78	0·70	0·00	0·38	0·92	107
108	Parsnips	150	13·3	67	87	20	80	753	60	17·6	0·76	80	0·77	0·33	0·58	0·96	108
*109	Potatoes	210	12·5	47	90	5	38	824	43	17·6	0·71	84	0·52	0·00	0·00	0·90	109
*110	Sugar beet	230	13·7	35	48	4	48	870	30	17·6	0·78	79	0·73	0·00	0·36	0·94	110
*111	Swede turnip	120	12·8	91	108	17	100	717	58	17·7	0·72	87	0·84	0·00	0·66	0·93	111
*112	Turnip	90	11·2	73	122	22	111	667	78	17·6	0·64	72	0·60	0·00	0·33	0·91	112
	2 Leaves of roots																
201	Artichoke tops	320	8·8	65	106	34	169	534	156	16·5	0·53	55	0·61	0·45	0·41	0·75	201
202	Carrot leaves	180	7·9	123	189	50	133	389	239	15·7	0·50	48	0·65	0·56	0·56	0·66	202
203	Kohlrabi leaves	140	10·2	141	207	29	121	529	114	17·5	0·58	65	0·68	0·50	0·56	0·80	203
204	Mangel leaves	110	9·0	146	218	36	145	418	182	16·6	0·54	57	0·67	0·50	0·57	0·76	204
205	Potato haulm	230	6·5	48	109	43	270	443	135	17·3	0·38	42	0·44	0·20	0·36	0·60	205
206	Sugar beet tops	160	9·9	88	125	31	100	531	212	15·4	0·64	62	0·70	0·60	0·69	0·83	206
*207	Turnip leaves	120	9·2	130	192	42	125	458	183	16·5	0·55	58	0·68	0·40	0·53	0·79	207
	3 Other green foods																
301	Cabbage, drumhead	110	10·4	100	136	36	182	536	109	17·5	0·59	66	0·73	0·50	0·70	0·78	301
302	Cabbage, open leaved	150	10·8	115	160	47	160	527	107	17·9	0·60	68	0·72	0·57	0·71	0·80	302
303	Comfrey	120	8·5	130	217	25	150	433	175	16·5	0·52	54	0·60	0·67	0·47	0·74	303
*304	Kale, thousandhead	160	11·1	106	137	25	200	531	106	17·4	0·64	71	0·77	0·50	0·56	0·90	304
305	Kale, marrow stem (unthinned)	140	11·0	123	157	36	179	493	136	17·2	0·64	69	0·78	0·60	0·64	0·88	305
306	Kale, marrow stem (singled)	140	11·0	114	150	21	179	521	129	16·9	0·65	70	0·76	0·67	0·60	0·89	306
307	Broccoli, purple sprouting	120	11·1	117	158	25	125	592	100	17·5	0·63	70	0·74	0·67	0·74	0·80	307
308	Mustard	150	9·0	126	193	27	193	493	93	17·9	0·50	57	0·65	0·50	0·52	0·68	308
309	Rape	140	9·5	144	200	57	250	400	93	18·7	0·51	59	0·72	0·63	0·54	0·68	309

76

Food number	Food name	Dry Matter Content g/kg	Metabolisable Energy MJ/kg DM	Digestible Crude Protein g/kg DM	Crude Protein	Ether Extract	Crude Fibre	N free Extract	Total Ash	Gross Energy MJ/kg DM	Q ME/GE	Digestible Organic Matter in Dry Matter DOMD%	Crude Protein	Ether Extract	Crude Fibre	N free Extract	Food number
	4 Cereals																
401	Barley in flower	250	10·0	46	68	16	316	536	64	17·7	0·56	66	0·68	0·60	0·64	0·75	401
402	Maize	190	8·8	53	89	26	289	532	63	18·1	0·49	57	0·59	0·60	0·55	0·64	402
403	Millet	130	7·9	54	100	15	315	477	92	17·4	0·45	52	0·54	0·50	0·54	0·61	403
404	Oats in flower	230	8·6	61	83	26	365	448	78	17·9	0·48	57	0·74	0·66	0·58	0·62	404
405	Rye in flower	230	9·5	88	126	39	322	439	74	18·4	0·52	62	0·70	0·56	0·65	0·68	405
	5 Grasses																
501	Pasture grass, close grazing; Non-rotational	200	12·1	225	265	55	130	445	105	18·6	0·65	75	0·85	0·64	0·81	0·87	501
502	Rotational, with 3 weekly intervals	200	12·1	185	225	65	155	465	90	18·9	0·64	75	0·82	0·61	0·81	0·86	502
503	Rotational, with monthly intervals	200	11·2	130	175	50	225	460	90	18·5	0·61	72	0·74	0·50	0·82	0·82	503
504	Pasture grass, extensive grazing Spring value, running off during summer	200	10·0	124	175	40	200	485	100	18·0	0·56	64	0·71	0·50	0·65	0·75	504
505	Winter pasturage (after close grazing allowing free growth from end July to December)	200	9·7	101	155	30	220	515	80	18·1	0·53	63	0·65	0·16	0·59	0·77	505
506	Rice grass	220	7·0	59	132	27	227	505	109	17·4	0·40	46	0·45	0·50	0·66	0·46	506
507	Ryegrass perennial post flowering	250	8·4	72	116	28	288	464	104	17·5	0·48	55	0·62	0·43	0·56	0·65	507
508	Ryegrass, Italian post flowering	250	8·7	84	136	40	248	464	112	17·7	0·49	55	0·62	0·50	0·58	0·66	508
509	Sorghum	200	8·0	60	105	30	310	485	70	18·1	0·44	53	0·57	0·33	0·53	0·60	509
510	Timothy, in flower	250	8·5	52	96	32	280	524	68	18·1	0·47	55	0·54	0·50	0·53	0·63	510
	6 Green legumes																
601	Alsike	150	8·8	141	220	40	300	340	100	18·4	0·48	56	0·64	0·67	0·49	0·71	601
602	Crimson clover	190	9·5	114	153	37	337	374	100	18·0	0·53	61	0·75	0·71	0·57	0·75	602
603	Red clover, beginning to flower	190	10·2	132	179	37	274	426	84	18·3	0·56	65	0·74	0·71	0·58	0·78	603
604	White clover, beginning to flower	190	9·0	152	237	42	232	374	116	18·1	0·50	57	0·64	0·63	0·60	0·68	604
605	Beans, beginning to flower	150	9·2	154	213	53	220	380	133	17·9	0·51	57	0·72	0·62	0·49	0·72	605
606	Kidney vetch	180	8·7	77	133	33	283	478	72	18·3	0·48	56	0·58	0·50	0·53	0·66	606
607	Lucerne, early flower	240	8·2	130	171	17	300	413	100	17·6	0·47	54	0·76	0·25	0·44	0·67	607
608	Lucerne, in bud	220	9·4	164	205	23	282	409	82	18·2	0·52	62	0·80	0·20	0·50	0·76	608
609	Lucerne, before bud	150	10·2	213	253	27	220	380	120	17·8	0·57	67	0·84	0·25	0·64	0·81	609
610	Peas, beginning to flower	170	8·5	140	206	35	353	335	71	18·8	0·45	56	0·68	0·50	0·50	0·66	610
611	Sainfoin, early flower	230	10·3	143	196	26	209	509	61	18·5	0·56	65	0·73	0·67	0·45	0·78	611
612	Sainfoin, full flower	250	8·4	116	176	24	236	500	64	18·3	0·46	54	0·66	0·50	0·46	0·61	612
613	Trefoil	200	9·0	121	175	40	285	420	80	18·5	0·49	57	0·69	0·50	0·49	0·70	613
614	Vetches, in flower	180	8·6	123	178	28	294	417	83	18·2	0·48	56	0·69	0·60	0·45	0·68	614

Food number	Food name	Dry Matter Content g/kg	Metabolisable Energy MJ/kg DM	Digestible Crude Protein g/kg DM	Crude Protein	Ether Extract	Crude Fibre	N free Extract	Total Ash	Gross Energy MJ/kg DM	Q (ME/GE)	Digestible Organic Matter in Dry Matter DOMD%	Crude Protein	Ether Extract	Crude Fibre	N free Extract	Food number
					Analysis of Dry Matter g/kg								Digestibility Coefficients (decimal)				

7 Miscellaneous

701	Brushwood	750	6·3	28	61	25	356	537	20	18·8	0·34	41	0·46	0·42	0·28	0·50	701
702	Buckwheat	160	9·1	100	156	38	262	475	69	18·5	0·49	59	0·64	0·50	0·57	0·67	702
703	Gorse	500	6·8	44	104	22	468	352	54	18·5	0·37	45	0·42	0·45	0·40	0·60	703
704	Heather	500	6·0	28	70	86	454	332	58	19·7	0·31	37	0·40	0·35	0·31	0·52	704
705	Artichoke tops (dried)	870	8·5	87	145	25	162	551	117	17·2	0·49	53	0·60	0·50	0·29	0·70	705
706	Elm leaves (dried)	880	10·3	132	181	33	98	567	122	17·3	0·59	65	0·73	0·24	0·57	0·81	706
707	Hop leaves and bine (dried)	890	8·2	90	140	39	273	426	121	17·6	0·47	51	0·64	0·72	0·31	0·71	707
708	Leaves of trees in July (dried)	840	9·1	74	125	36	169	587	83	17·9	0·51	55	0·59	0·80	0·37	0·66	708
709	Nettles (dried)	890	10·4	145	207	87	119	429	158	18·1	0·57	61	0·70	0·64	0·57	0·79	709
710	Poplar leaves in October (dried)	840	9·7	72	129	104	207	471	89	19·4	0·50	53	0·56	0·79	0·32	0·66	710

8a Silage—Clamp

801	Alsike	250	8·6	80	136	72	272	436	84	18·9	0·45	51	0·59	0·67	0·50	0·57	801
802	Clover (red)	220	8·8	135	205	55	300	327	114	18·4	0·48	56	0·66	0·54	0·53	0·72	802
803	Grass (very high digestibility)	200	10·2	116	170	40	300	390	100	18·1	0·57	67	0·68	0·67	0·81	0·72	803
804	Grass (high digestibility)	200	9·3	107	170	40	305	390	95	18·2	0·51	61	0·63	0·62	0·76	0·63	804
805	Grass (moderate digestibility)	200	8·8	102	160	35	340	375	90	18·2	0·48	58	0·64	0·57	0·73	0·56	805
806	Grass (low digestibility)	200	7·6	98	160	35	380	345	80	18·4	0·41	52	0·61	0·35	0·69	0·42	806
807	Lucerne	250	8·5	113	168	84	296	352	100	19·1	0·45	52	0·67	0·48	0·42	0·69	807
808	Maize	210	10·8	70	110	57	233	538	62	18·8	0·57	65	0·64	0·90	0·68	0·69	808
809	Mangel leaves	220	6·9	88	132	50	145	450	223	15·8	0·44	43	0·67	0·40	0·55	0·54	809
810	Marrowstem kale	160	9·8	95	125	31	231	456	156	16·6	0·59	65	0·76	0·00	0·74	0·85	810
811	Mustard	150	9·6	107	167	27	253	400	153	16·8	0·57	60	0·64	1·00	0·50	0·85	811
812	Oats (green)	240	8·0	47	79	33	358	454	75	18·1	0·44	53	0·60	0·55	0·60	0·55	812
813	Overheated ryegrass and clover	320	7·1	16	134	34	319	422	91	18·0	0·39	45	0·12	0·73	0·55	0·56	813
814	Pea haulm & pods (canning)	210	8·7	95	167	67	290	276	200	16·9	0·51	51	0·57	0·93	0·56	0·69	814
815	Pea pods (canning)	280	10·6	85	129	36	307	464	64	18·5	0·58	67	0·66	0·90	0·65	0·77	815
816	Potatoes	270	11·8	39	81	19	26	822	52	17·6	0·67	74	0·48	0·20	0·00	0·85	816
817	Potato haulm	250	6·4	49	128	108	176	364	224	17·1	0·38	36	0·38	0·44	0·39	0·55	817
818	Rye	130	8·3	71	123	38	338	431	69	18·5	0·45	55	0·58	0·38	0·60	0·60	818
819	Sainfoin	240	8·4	124	179	63	333	342	83	19·0	0·44	52	0·69	0·50	0·42	0·67	819
820	Sugar beet pulp (wet)	120	9·7	42	83	17	200	625	75	17·5	0·55	62	0·50	0·50	0·50	0·75	820
821	Sugar beet tops	230	7·9	65	104	30	148	396	322	13·4	0·59	50	0·62	0·50	0·73	0·80	821
822	Sugar beet tops and pulp	160	11·3	100	150	38	131	556	125	17·3	0·65	70	0·67	0·67	0·81	0·85	822
823	Sunflowers	220	8·4	51	95	45	305	450	105	17·8	0·47	53	0·53	0·67	0·49	0·66	823
824	Turnip tops	170	8·4	88	124	35	159	353	329	13·5	0·62	52	0·71	0·83	0·68	0·83	824
825	Vetch and oats	270	9·6	82	126	44	293	456	81	18·3	0·52	60	0·65	0·73	0·58	0·70	825

78

Food number	Food name	Dry Matter Content g/kg	Metabolisable Energy MJ/kg DM	Digestible Crude Protein g/kg DM	Crude Protein	Ether Extract	Crude Fibre	N free Extract	Total Ash	Gross Energy MJ/kg DM	Q [ME/GE]	Digestible Organic Matter in Dry Matter DOMD%	Crude Protein	Ether Extract	Crude Fibre	N free Extract	Food number
\multicolumn{17}{	l	}{**8b Silage—Tower**}	
826	Barley (whole crop)	400	9·6	50	95	22	250	570	63	18·0	0·54	62	0·53	0·61	0·53	0·74	826
827	Grass (very high digestibility)	400	10·4	121	170	38	313	383	97	18·1	0·57	68	0·71	0·65	0·80	0·74	827
828	Grass (high digestibility)	400	9·3	87	142	28	313	433	85	18·0	0·52	61	0·61	0·67	0·73	0·64	828
829	Wheat (whole crop)	400	8·4	36	78	17	300	563	42	18·2	0·46	55	0·47	0·56	0·43	0·66	829
\multicolumn{17}{	l	}{**9 Hay**}	
901	Barley (just past milk stage)	850	8·8	54	81	22	289	533	74	17·7	0·50	58	0·67	0·42	0·62	0·63	901
902	Clover, crimson	850	8·2	100	144	29	314	426	87	18·0	0·46	54	0·70	0·40	0·47	0·65	902
903	Clover, red very good	850	9·6	128	184	39	266	428	84	18·4	0·52	61	0·70	0·64	0·50	0·75	903
904	Clover, red good	850	8·9	103	161	35	287	445	72	18·5	0·48	57	0·64	0·57	0·47	0·70	904
905	Clover, red poor	850	7·8	67	131	25	340	445	60	18·4	0·42	50	0·51	0·48	0·40	0·65	905
906	Clover, red damaged	850	6·9	73	141	18	394	364	84	17·9	0·38	46	0·52	0·47	0·40	0·60	906
907	Grass (very high digestibility)	850	10·1	90	132	20	291	473	85	17·7	0·57	67	0·68	0·37	0·76	0·75	907
908	Grass (high digestibility)	850	9·0	58	101	16	320	480	82	17·6	0·51	61	0·57	0·30	0·70	0·67	908
909	Grass (moderate digestibility)	850	8·4	39	85	16	328	496	74	17·7	0·48	57	0·46	0·27	0·61	0·65	909
910	Grass (low digestibility)	850	7·5	45	92	16	366	456	69	17·8	0·42	51	0·49	0·27	0·56	0·56	910
911	Grass (very low digestibility)	850	7·0	38	88	16	340	478	78	17·6	0·40	47	0·43	0·35	0·54	0·51	911
912	Lucerne, before flowering	850	8·3	143	193	28	321	371	87	18·2	0·46	54	0·74	0·46	0·42	0·68	912
913	Lucerne, half flower	850	8·2	166	225	13	302	365	95	17·9	0·46	55	0·74	0·00	0·48	0·66	913
914	Lucerne, full flower	850	7·7	116	171	31	353	349	96	18·1	0·43	51	0·68	0·46	0·45	0·62	914
915	Millet hay	850	8·4	71	125	26	339	445	66	18·2	0·46	56	0·57	0·41	0·60	0·61	915
916	Mineral deficient hay (mainly purple molinia and brown bent)	850	6·4	63	129	22	344	469	35	18·7	0·34	44	0·49	0·11	0·55	0·39	916
917	Oats, milk stage	850	7·8	52	94	31	324	473	79	18·0	0·43	50	0·55	0·62	0·52	0·56	917
918	Rice grass, poor	850	7·0	31	79	16	306	499	100	17·2	0·41	47	0·39	0·36	0·63	0·49	918
919	Rye, before flowering	850	9·5	85	121	29	332	455	62	18·4	0·52	62	0·70	0·60	0·60	0·70	919
920	Sainfoin, before flowering	850	9·2	129	182	38	296	404	80	18·5	0·50	58	0·71	0·66	0·43	0·74	920
921	Sainfoin, in flower	850	9·0	115	158	31	335	389	87	18·1	0·50	58	0·73	0·62	0·42	0·78	921
922	Trefoil	850	8·8	139	184	40	292	395	89	18·4	0·48	56	0·76	0·47	0·44	0·70	922
923	Vetches, beginning to flower	850	8·8	181	238	27	281	342	112	17·9	0·49	57	0·76	0·61	0·54	0·65	923
924	Vetches, full flower	850	8·0	113	171	29	306	394	100	17·9	0·45	52	0·66	0·60	0·50	0·60	924
925	Vetches, and oats (vetches in flower)	850	8·1	77	138	39	288	433	102	17·9	0·46	52	0·56	0·52	0·51	0·64	925
926	Wheat, milk stage	850	8·5	36	66	19	293	551	72	17·6	0·48	56	0·55	0·56	0·58	0·62	926

Food number	Food name	Dry Matter Content g/kg	Metabolisable Energy MJ/kg DM	Digestible Crude Protein g/kg DM	Crude Protein	E her Ex ract	Crude Fibre	N free Extract	Total Ash	Gross Energy MJ/kg DM	Q (ME/GE)	Digestible Organic Matter in Dry Matter DOMD%	Crude Protein	Ether Extract	Crude Fibre	N free Extract	Food number
10 Dried grasses and legumes
1001	Grass, very leafy	900	10.8	113	161	28	217	471	123	17.3	0.62	70	0.70	0.58	0.83	0.83	1001
1002	Grass, leafy	900	10.6	136	187	38	213	460	102	18.0	0.59	68	0.73	0.61	0.79	0.77	1002
1003	Grass, early flower	900	9.7	97	154	28	258	453	107	17.6	0.55	64	0.63	0.49	0.75	0.73	1003
1004	Lucerne, just in bud	900	9.4	174	244	22	198	400	126	17.7	0.53	60	0.71	0.45	0.53	0.78	1004
1005	Lucerne, early flower	900	8.7	128	178	27	269	414	112	17.6	0.49	57	0.72	0.29	0.46	0.74	1005
1006	Lucerne leaf meal (Amer.)	900	9.3	179	236	21	176	446	122	17.4	0.54	61	0.76	0.00	0.49	0.78	1006
11 Straws and chaff
1101	Barley straw, spring	860	7.3	9	38	21	394	493	53	18.0	0.40	49	0.24	0.33	0.54	0.53	1101
1102	Barley straw, winter	860	5.8	8	37	6	488	392	66	17.8	0.32	39	0.22	0.29	0.38	0.50	1102
1103	Bean straw (including pods)	860	7.4	26	52	9	501	384	53	18.0	0.41	50	0.49	0.63	0.43	0.67	1103
1104	Buckwheat straw	860	6.6	27	57	4	455	413	62	17.9	0.37	45	0.47	0.42	0.45	0.52	1104
1105	Clover straw, red	840	5.6	48	108	21	531	271	68	18.3	0.31	38	0.44	0.33	0.37	0.49	1105
1106	Maize straw	850	7.3	20	59	8	461	406	56	18.1	0.40	51	0.34	0.32	0.60	0.50	1106
1107	Oat straw, spring	860	6.7	11	34	22	394	493	57	18.0	0.38	46	0.34	0.33	0.54	0.46	1107
1108	Oat straw, winter	860	6.8	9	22	7	402	501	57	17.8	0.38	46	0.40	0.33	0.57	0.44	1108
1109	Pea straw	860	6.5	50	105	9	410	390	77	17.9	0.36	43	0.48	0.44	0.39	0.55	1109
1110	Rape straw	840	6.5	21	30	4	450	461	45	18.0	0.36	44	0.72	0.42	0.37	0.53	1110
1111	Rye straw, spring	860	6.2	7	37	9	429	485	30	18.4	0.33	42	0.19	0.50	0.47	0.41	1111
1112	Rye straw, winter	860	6.3	7	36	6	465	437	45	18.1	0.35	43	0.19	0.50	0.51	0.41	1112
1113	Soya bean straw	840	7.5	44	88	24	311	456	121	17.0	0.44	48	0.50	0.60	0.38	0.66	1113
1114	Tare or vetch straw	860	6.3	48	105	20	472	342	62	18.3	0.34	42	0.46	0.47	0.40	0.52	1114
1115	Wheat straw, spring	860	5.6	1	34	5	417	463	71	17.6	0.32	39	0.03	0.31	0.50	0.37	1115
1116	Wheat straw, winter	860	5.7	1	24	5	426	473	62	17.7	0.32	39	0.03	0.31	0.50	0.37	1116
1117	Linseed chaff	880	5.0	16	40	39	460	395	66	18.3	0.27	32	0.40	0.50	0.30	0.37	1117
1118	Lupin pods	870	7.4	39	103	8	334	485	69	17.7	0.42	50	0.38	0.29	0.48	0.61	1118
1119	Millet chaff and husks	880	5.2	19	55	25	464	330	127	17.0	0.31	35	0.35	0.32	0.37	0.47	1119
1120	Oat chaff, spring	860	6.4	26	70	24	265	521	120	16.9	0.38	41	0.37	0.48	0.45	0.49	1120
1121	Rice husks	900	2.5	5	42	16	421	364	157	16.1	0.15	15	0.11	0.64	0.01	0.35	1121
1122	Rye chaff	860	5.8	13	41	15	515	340	90	17.4	0.33	41	0.31	0.31	0.50	0.39	1122
1123	Soya bean pods	890	8.6	30	67	17	340	482	93	17.3	0.50	56	0.44	0.53	0.51	0.73	1123
1124	Wheat chaff	860	5.9	13	43	14	322	495	126	16.5	0.36	39	0.30	0.29	0.48	0.45	1124

Food number	Food name	Dry Matter Content g/kg	Metab-olisable Energy MJ/kg DM	Diges-tible Crude Protein g/kg DM	Crude Protein	Ether Extract	Crude Fibre	N free Extract	Total Ash	Gross Energy MJ/kg DM	Q ME/GE	Digestible Organic Matter in Dry Matter DOMD%	Crude Protein	Ether Extract	Crude Fibre	N free Extract	Food number
12a Grains and seeds—cereals
*1201	Barley	860	13.7	82	108	17	53	795	26	18.3	0.75	86	0.76	0.80	0.56	0.92	1201
1202	Sorghum	860	13.4	87	108	43	21	801	27	18.8	0.72	81	0.80	0.79	0.53	0.85	1202
*1203	Maize	860	14.2	78	98	42	24	823	13	19.0	0.75	87	0.80	0.61	0.36	0.92	1203
1204	Millet	860	11.3	92	121	44	93	698	44	18.7	0.61	68	0.76	0.80	0.33	0.75	1204
*1205	Oats	860	11.5	84	109	49	121	688	33	19.0	0.61	68	0.77	0.83	0.25	0.77	1205
1206	Rice (polished)	860	15.0	67	77	5	17	892	9	18.0	0.83	94	0.87	0.50	0.47	0.97	1206
1207	Rye	860	14.0	110	133	20	22	802	23	18.4	0.76	87	0.83	0.65	0.53	0.92	1207
*1208	Wheat	860	14.0	105	124	19	26	810	21	18.4	0.76	87	0.84	0.63	0.47	0.92	1208
12b Legumes
1209	Beans, field spring	860	12.8	248	314	15	80	551	40	19.0	0.67	81	0.79	0.80	0.58	0.91	1209
1210	Beans, field winter	860	12.8	209	265	15	90	591	40	18.8	0.68	81	0.79	0.80	0.58	0.91	1210
1211	Beans, butter	860	12.6	175	265	13	42	631	49	18.5	0.68	80	0.66	0.64	0.62	0.93	1211
1212	Gram	860	12.4	173	263	13	57	610	57	18.4	0.67	78	0.66	0.64	0.57	0.93	1212
1213	Lentils	860	13.6	255	297	22	40	607	35	19.1	0.71	85	0.86	0.63	0.53	0.93	1213
1214	Lupins, sweet (yellow)	860	13.2	432	480	63	120	285	52	20.8	0.64	81	0.90	0.84	0.91	0.76	1214
1215	Lupins, sweet (blue)	860	13.3	346	388	67	83	423	38	20.6	0.65	81	0.89	0.81	0.97	0.77	1215
1216	Peas	860	13.4	225	262	19	63	624	33	18.9	0.71	85	0.86	0.63	0.46	0.93	1216
1217	Vetches	860	13.6	264	300	20	69	574	37	19.1	0.71	85	0.88	0.88	0.65	0.92	1217
12c Oil seeds
1218	Beech mast	900	15.2	121	149	308	208	288	48	25.0	0.61	66	0.81	0.88	0.40	0.66	1218
1219	Cottonseed, Egyptian	900	14.1	147	216	261	233	236	54	24.1	0.59	67	0.68	0.87	0.76	0.50	1219
1220	Cottonseed, Bombay	900	13.1	135	196	212	219	327	47	23.0	0.57	65	0.69	0.87	0.76	0.50	1220
1221	Cottonseed, Brazilian	900	14.1	159	233	256	188	276	48	24.2	0.58	66	0.68	0.88	0.76	0.50	1221
1222	Groundnuts or peanuts	900	21.1	256	284	478	28	187	23	29.7	0.71	85	0.90	0.90	0.08	0.84	1222
1223	Hemp seed	900	17.5	150	200	359	164	231	46	26.4	0.66	76	0.75	0.90	0.60	0.80	1223
1224	Linseed	900	19.3	208	260	392	59	248	41	27.4	0.71	80	0.80	0.95	0.33	0.80	1224
1225	Palm nut kernels	900	23.0	87	92	532	63	292	20	30.1	0.76	88	0.94	0.95	0.60	0.84	1225
1226	Rape seed	900	21.0	172	212	484	63	194	46	29.2	0.72	80	0.81	0.95	0.25	0.80	1226
1227	Sesame seed	900	20.8	195	217	499	67	159	59	29.3	0.71	77	0.90	0.95	0.22	0.56	1227
1228	Soya bean	900	14.9	328	369	194	46	339	52	23.1	0.64	75	0.89	0.90	0.42	0.68	1228
1229	Sunflower seed	900	16.6	138	153	350	303	157	37	26.3	0.63	68	0.90	0.95	0.34	0.71	1229

81

Food number	Food name	Dry Matter Content g/kg	Metabolisable Energy MJ/kg DM	Digestible Crude Protein g/kg DM	Crude Protein	E her Ex ract	Crude Fibre	N free Extract	Total Ash	Gross Energy MJ/kg DM	Q [ME/GE]	Digestible Organic Matter in Dry Matter DOMD%	Crude Protein	Ether Extract	Crude Fibre	N free Extract	Food number
	12d Miscellaneous seeds																
1230	Acorns, fresh	500	13·6	54	66	48	136	726	24	18·9	0·72	83	0·82	0·79	0·60	0·90	1230
1231	Acorns, dried	860	13·6	55	67	49	136	724	23	18·9	0·72	83	0·81	0·80	0·60	0·90	1231
1232	Buckwheat	860	10·6	99	131	30	167	638	33	18·7	0·57	65	0·75	0·73	0·24	0·77	1232
1233	Corozo nut (vegetable ivory)	900	13·6	21	51	10	77	850	12	18·1	0·75	86	0·41	0·33	0·65	0·93	1233
1234	Horse chestnut, fresh	500	12·1	50	84	30	50	804	32	18·3	0·66	74	0·60	0·80	0·32	0·81	1234
1235	Horse chestnut, dry	860	11·2	50	85	29	51	803	31	18·3	0·61	68	0·59	0·83	0·29	0·74	1235
1236	Locust beans (pods plus seeds)	860	13·8	47	69	15	76	812	29	18·0	0·77	87	0·69	0·54	0·58	0·95	1236
1237	Lucerne seed meal	880	14·1	316	376	119	92	363	50	21·5	0·65	79	0·84	0·86	0·62	0·87	1237
1238	Mangel seed	880	7·5	83	139	51	386	334	80	19·0	0·40	46	0·60	0·60	0·35	0·62	1238
1239	Red clover seed meal	880	13·4	313	373	39	106	357	76	20·4	0·66	78	0·84	0·87	0·82	0·86	1239
1240	Rye grass seed meal (perennial and Italian)	880	11·5	72	108	22	105	719	47	18·1	0·64	71	0·67	0·84	0·21	0·83	1240
1241	Sainfoin seed meal (unmilled seed)	880	11·6	258	300	58	203	383	45	20·2	0·57	69	0·86	0·88	0·41	0·75	1241
1242	Sugar beet seed	880	7·1	82	136	51	451	277	74	19·1	0·37	44	0·60	0·60	0·34	0·60	1242
	13 Oil cakes and meals																
1301	Beech mast cake, shelled	900	12·6	357	406	94	76	337	88	20·4	0·62	72	0·88	0·90	0·24	0·76	1301
1302	Beech mast cake, unshelled	900	8·9	162	217	101	299	328	56	20·6	0·43	47	0·75	0·91	0·16	0·51	1302
1303	Castor bean meal (de-toxicated)	900	6·2	263	324	6	412	177	71	19·0	0·32	39	0·81	0·93	0·09	0·43	1303
1304	Coconut cake	900	13·0	184	236	81	127	491	66	19·7	0·66	75	0·78	0·97	0·63	0·83	1304
1305	Coconut cake meal	900	12·7	174	220	76	153	479	72	19·5	0·65	74	0·79	0·94	0·63	0·83	1305
1306	Cotton cake, Bombay	900	8·5	178	231	54	248	401	66	19·3	0·44	50	0·77	0·93	0·20	0·54	1306
1307	Cotton cake, Brazilian	900	8·9	234	304	51	280	304	50	20·1	0·44	51	0·77	0·92	0·21	0·54	1307
1308	Cotton cake, Egyptian	900	8·7	203	263	57	242	372	66	19·5	0·45	51	0·77	0·94	0·21	0·54	1308
1309	Cotton cake, decorticated	900	12·3	393	457	39	87	293	74	20·8	0·59	70	0·86	0·92	0·28	0·67	1309
1310	Cotton cake, semi-decorticated	900	11·4	366	426	69	143	297	66	20·4	0·56	66	0·86	0·93	0·27	0·66	1310
1311	Ground nut cake, decorticated	900	12·9	449	504	67	72	293	63	20·7	0·62	76	0·89	0·90	0·08	0·85	1311
1312	Ground nut cake, undecorticated	900	11·4	310	337	101	256	243	63	20·9	0·55	63	0·92	0·90	0·11	0·84	1312
1313	Ground nut meal, decorticated extracted	900	11·7	491	552	8	88	289	63	19·6	0·60	75	0·89	0·86	0·08	0·85	1313
1314	Ground nut meal, undecorticated extracted	900	9·2	316	343	31	273	316	47	19·5	0·47	58	0·92	0·79	0·11	0·69	1314
1315	Hemp seed cake	900	9·0	255	344	97	268	204	87	20·5	0·44	48	0·74	0·90	0·08	0·58	1315
1316	Hemp seed meal	900	6·9	296	394	19	291	190	106	18·6	0·37	43	0·75	0·77	0·08	0·53	1316
1317	Kapok cake	900	8·7	232	313	31	299	233	73	20·3	0·43	48	0·74	0·91	0·20	0·50	1317

Food number	Food name	Dry Matter Content g/kg	Metabolisable Energy MJ/kg DM	Digestible Crude Protein g/kg DM	Crude Protein	Ether Extract	Crude Fibre	N free Extract	Total Ash	Gross Energy MJ/kg DM	Q (ME/GE)	Digestible Organic Matter in Dry Matter DOMD%	Crude Protein	Ether Extract	Crude Fibre	N free Extract	Food number
1318	Linseed cake, English made	900	13·4	286	332	107	102	400	59	20·9	0·64	75	0·86	0·92	0·49	0·80	1318
1319	Linseed cake, foreign	900	12·9	305	354	77	104	402	62	20·3	0·63	75	0·86	0·93	0·50	0·80	1319
1320	Linseed meal, extracted	900	11·9	348	404	36	102	384	73	19·4	0·62	74	0·86	0·90	0·50	0·80	1320
1321	Media cake	900	9·6	250	358	117	233	207	86	21·0	0·46	51	0·70	0·80	0·20	0·60	1321
1322	Niger cake	900	10·5	292	364	66	203	262	104	19·4	0·54	62	0·80	0·81	0·27	0·84	1322
1323	Olive cake	900	12·7	69	71	201	338	329	61	22·1	0·57	60	0·97	0·95	0·33	0·70	1323
1324	Palm kernel cake	900	12·8	196	216	68	150	522	44	19·8	0·65	76	0·91	0·88	0·38	0·85	1324
1325	Palm kernel meal, extracted	900	12·2	204	227	10	167	552	44	18·5	0·66	78	0·90	0·89	0·50	0·88	1325
1326	Poppy seed cake	900	11·3	322	408	108	92	240	152	19·6	0·58	62	0·79	0·93	0·49	0·64	1326
1327	Rape cake	900	11·4	322	388	106	91	280	136	19·8	0·58	64	0·83	0·79	0·08	0·80	1327
1328	Rape meal, extracted	900	10·9	343	413	34	104	366	82	19·2	0·57	67	0·83	0·77	0·11	0·80	1328
1329	Sesame cake, English	900	13·0	442	491	131	49	231	98	21·5	0·61	70	0·90	0·90	0·31	0·56	1329
1330	Sesame cake, French	900	11·7	371	412	121	187	183	97	21·1	0·56	64	0·90	0·90	0·31	0·56	1330
1331	Sesame meal, extracted	900	10·4	444	493	26	82	284	114	18·8	0·55	65	0·90	0·92	0·31	0·56	1331
1332	Soya bean cake	900	13·3	454	504	66	60	308	62	20·7	0·64	79	0·90	0·91	0·72	0·77	1332
1333	Soya bean meal, extracted	900	12·3	453	503	17	58	360	62	19·5	0·63	79	0·90	0·93	0·71	0·77	1333
1334	Sunflower cake, decorticated	900	13·3	372	413	152	134	226	74	22·1	0·60	71	0·90	0·88	0·30	0·71	1334
1335	Sunflower cake, undecorticated	900	9·5	185	206	80	323	311	80	19·6	0·48	53	0·90	0·88	0·18	0·71	1335
1336	Sunflower meal, extracted	900	10·4	381	423	11	181	312	72	19·0	0·54	67	0·90	0·90	0·30	0·71	1336
1337	Walnut cake	900	14·7	364	404	141	77	319	59	22·0	0·67	79	0·90	0·95	0·25	0·85	1337

14 Feedingstuffs of animal orgin

Food number	Food name	Dry Matter Content g/kg	Metabolisable Energy MJ/kg DM	Digestible Crude Protein g/kg DM	Crude Protein	Ether Extract	Crude Fibre	N free Extract	Total Ash	Gross Energy MJ/kg DM	Q (ME/GE)	Digestible Organic Matter in Dry Matter DOMD%	Crude Protein	Ether Extract	Crude Fibre	N free Extract	Food number
1401	Blood meal	900	13·2	848	942	9	0	18	31	22·0	0·60	86	0·90	1·00	0·00	0·00	1401
1402	Fish meal, white	900	11·1	631	701	40	0	18	241	17·8	0·62	68	0·90	0·94	0·00	0·80	1402
1403	Greaves	900	18·2	615	648	281	0	0	71	26·1	0·70	87	0·95	0·92	0·00	0·00	1403
1404	Pure meat meal	900	16·3	753	810	148	0	0	42	24·3	0·67	89	0·93	0·95	0·00	0·00	1404
1405	Feeding meat meal (high fat)	900	13·3	624	663	121	0	6	210	20·0	0·66	74	0·94	0·89	0·00	1·00	1405
1406	Feeding meat meal (low fat)	900	11·1	631	717	31	0	43	209	18·2	0·61	70	0·88	0·83	0·00	0·98	1406
1407	Meat and bone meal (high protein)	900	9·7	465	597	50	0	62	291	16·6	0·58	57	0·78	0·95	0·00	0·98	1407
1408	Meat and bone meal (medium protein)	900	7·9	411	527	44	0	17	412	14·0	0·57	47	0·78	0·95	0·00	0·98	1408
1409	Milk, cows' whole	128	20·2	250	266	305	0	375	55	25·0	0·81	93	0·94	1·00	0·00	1·00	1409
1410	Milk, buttermilk	92	15·7	368	391	87	0	446	76	20·3	0·77	90	0·94	1·00	0·00	1·00	1410
1411	Milk, separated	94	14·1	350	372	11	0	532	85	18·3	0·77	89	0·94	1·00	0·00	1·00	1411
1412	Milk, skimmed, deep set	97	14·8	339	361	41	0	515	82	19·0	0·78	90	0·94	1·00	0·00	1·00	1412
1413	Milk, skimmed, shallow set	100	15·3	329	350	70	0	500	80	19·6	0·78	90	0·94	1·00	0·00	1·00	1413
1414	Milk, whey	66	14·5	91	106	30	0	758	106	17·0	0·85	88	0·86	1·00	0·00	1·00	1414

15 By-products

Food number	Food name	Dry Matter Content g/kg	Metab-olisable Energy MJ/kg DM	Diges-tible Crude Protein g/kg DM	Crude Protein	Ether Extract	Crude Fibre	N free Extract	Total Ash	Gross Energy MJ/kg DM	Q (ME/GE)	Digestible Organic Matter in Dry Matter DOMD%	Crude Protein	Ether Extract	Crude Fibre	N free Extract	Food number
*1501	Apple pomace, fresh	250	8·4	28	60	44	184	656	56	18·3	0·46	51	0·47	0·45	0·00	0·70	1501
1502	Apple pomace, dried	900	7·7	18	46	40	308	587	20	19·0	0·41	47	0·40	0·49	0·06	0·70	1502
1503	Fine barley dust	860	13·5	101	136	26	52	750	36	18·4	0·73	83	0·74	0·91	0·24	0·92	1503
*1504	Barley, brewers' grains, fresh	220	10·0	149	205	64	186	500	45	19·6	0·51	59	0·73	0·86	0·39	0·62	1504
1505	Barley, brewers' grains, ensiled	280	10·0	149	204	64	185	500	43	19·7	0·51	59	0·73	0·86	0·39	0·62	1505
1506	Barley, brewers' grains, dried	900	10·3	145	204	71	169	512	43	19·8	0·52	60	0·71	0·88	0·48	0·60	1506
1507	Barley, distillers' grains, fresh	250	11·8	237	320	116	136	396	32	21·6	0·55	65	0·74	0·87	0·47	0·62	1507
1508	Barley, distillers' grains, dried	900	12·1	214	301	126	110	443	20	21·9	0·55	65	0·71	0·88	0·48	0·62	1508
1509	Barley, ale and porter grains, fresh	250	10·2	178	240	76	212	428	44	20·2	0·51	59	0·74	0·86	0·39	0·62	1509
1510	Barley, ale and porter grains, dried	900	10·3	153	219	74	194	477	36	20·1	0·51	60	0·70	0·88	0·48	0·60	1510
1511	Barley malt culms	900	11·2	222	271	22	156	471	80	18·4	0·61	72	0·82	0·75	0·91	0·73	1511
1512	Bean husks (chaff or hulls)	900	9·4	0	40	2	488	421	49	17·8	0·53	67	0·00	1·00	0·88	0·57	1512
1513	Broad bean pod meal	900	10·4	112	167	11	178	571	73	17·7	0·59	67	0·67	0·60	0·58	0·79	1513
1514	Fodder-cellulose (from wheat straw by paper process)	900	10·3	0	3	6	798	162	31	18·5	0·56	79	0·00	0·00	0·91	0·38	1514
1515	Flax chaff (containing about 10 per cent seed)	860	6·5	55	92	57	369	402	80	18·6	0·35	40	0·60	0·74	0·46	0·32	1515
1516	Hominy chop, high grade	900	14·7	78	118	89	49	716	29	19·9	0·74	84	0·66	0·91	0·75	0·90	1516
1517	Hominy chop, low grade	900	14·1	70	106	69	94	701	30	19·4	0·73	83	0·66	0·90	0·75	0·90	1517
1518	Hops, spent, fresh	250	6·3	52	172	76	236	456	60	19·6	0·32	35	0·30	0·63	0·17	0·47	1518
1519	Hops, spent, dried	900	6·4	53	172	77	236	443	72	19·4	0·33	36	0·31	0·65	0·17	0·48	1519
1520	Horse-chestnut meal (alcohol-extracted)	900	10·1	0	73	74	80	746	27	19·4	0·52	58	0·00	0·60	0·00	0·72	1520
1521	Horse-chestnut meal (water extracted)	900	9·9	0	78	78	84	736	24	19·6	0·51	57	0·00	0·66	0·00	0·70	1521
1522	Lentil husks (chaff or hulls)	900	9·0	15	127	8	291	539	36	18·3	0·49	60	0·12	1·00	0·67	0·70	1522
1523	Maize, flaked	900	15·0	106	110	49	17	814	10	19·2	0·78	92	0·96	0·47	0·33	0·97	1523
1524	Maize germ meal, high fat	900	14·9	116	146	140	46	628	41	21·0	0·71	80	0·80	0·92	0·61	0·84	1524
1525	Maize germ meal, low fat	900	13·2	90	112	36	34	779	39	18·4	0·71	80	0·80	0·92	0·61	0·84	1525
1526	Maize meal, degermed, cooked	900	15·6	99	104	17	14	856	9	18·5	0·85	97	0·95	0·87	0·92	0·99	1526
1527	Maize bran	900	12·5	62	96	47	132	704	21	19·1	0·66	75	0·65	0·86	0·33	0·86	1527
1528	Maize, gluten feed	900	13·5	223	262	38	35	633	28	19·4	0·70	83	0·85	0·79	0·71	0·87	1528
*1529	Maize, gluten meal	900	14·2	339	394	52	23	518	12	20·7	0·69	85	0·86	0·94	0·00	0·90	1529
*1530	Maize, malt culms	860	15·1	201	240	167	67	457	69	21·6	0·70	80	0·84	0·86	0·78	0·88	1530
1531	Maize, feeding meal from corn flour	900	13·8	188	227	49	56	658	11	19·8	0·69	84	0·83	0·80	0·66	0·87	1531

84

Food number	Food name	Dry Matter Content g/kg	Metabolisable Energy MJ/kg DM	Digestible Crude Protein g/kg DM	Crude Protein	Ether Extract	Crude Fibre	N free Extract	Total Ash	Gross Energy MJ/kg DM	Q (ME/GE)	Digestible Organic Matter in Dry Matter DOMD%	Crude Protein	Ether Extract	Crude Fibre	N free Extract	Food number
1532	Maize, starch feed	900	14.1	211	251	76	83	580	10	20.6	0.69	83	0.84	0.90	0.72	0.85	1532
1533	Malt, dry	900	12.9	118	148	33	97	694	28	18.8	0.68	80	0.80	0.77	0.50	0.87	1533
1534	Oat bran ⎫ from preparation	900	8.8	44	89	40	242	562	67	18.2	0.49	55	0.50	0.56	0.37	0.70	1534
1535	Oat-meal ⎬ of oat-meal	900	12.4	131	174	73	18	712	22	19.9	0.62	72	0.75	0.81	0.50	0.73	1535
1536	Oat husks ⎭	900	4.9	0	21	11	351	574	42	17.8	0.28	33	0.00	0.40	0.33	0.36	1536
1537	Pea husks (chaff or hulls)	860	12.5	41	60	8	545	355	31	18.4	0.68	88	0.68	0.71	0.94	0.90	1537
1538	Pea pod meal (from canning industry)	900	10.7	108	150	13	169	604	63	17.9	0.60	69	0.72	0.67	0.63	0.77	1538
1539	Potato sludge	860	9.9	0	40	1	102	793	64	16.9	0.58	62	0.00	0.00	0.13	0.77	1539
1540	Potato slump	900	6.6	135	270	41	106	453	130	17.8	0.37	40	0.50	0.49	0.21	0.50	1540
1541	Potato pulp (dry)	860	10.8	0	40	1	102	793	64	16.9	0.64	68	0.00	0.00	0.24	0.83	1541
1542	Potato cossettes (meal)	900	12.4	54	98	6	22	834	40	17.6	0.70	78	0.55	0.00	0.50	0.86	1542
1543	Potato flakes	900	13.3	42	91	3	23	840	43	17.5	0.76	84	0.46	0.00	0.48	0.94	1543
1544	Potato slices	900	13.1	45	104	2	18	832	44	17.5	0.75	83	0.43	0.00	0.50	0.93	1544
1545	Rice meal	900	12.7	82	141	150	70	544	94	20.3	0.62	66	0.58	0.85	0.25	0.79	1545
1546	Rice sludge, dried	860	13.6	250	305	24	13	642	16	19.5	0.70	85	0.82	0.48	0.64	0.91	1546
1547	Rye bran	880	11.2	143	191	35	59	664	51	18.6	0.60	68	0.75	0.77	0.33	0.74	1547
1548	Seaweed meal (dried): *Laminaria*	860	8.8	73	136	13	102	548	201	15.3	0.58	56	0.54	0.82	0.73	0.73	1548
1549	Seaweed meal (dried): *Fucus*	860	8.8	0	58	48	106	605	184	16.0	0.55	51	0.00	0.95	0.66	0.66	1549
1550	Sugar beet pulp, pressed	180	12.7	66	106	6	206	644	39	18.0	0.71	84	0.63	0.00	0.90	0.91	1550
1551	Sugar beet pulp, dried	900	12.7	59	99	7	203	657	34	18.0	0.71	84	0.60	0.00	0.89	0.91	1551
1552	Sugar beet pulp, molassed	900	12.2	61	106	6	144	662	82	17.1	0.71	79	0.58	0.00	0.89	0.91	1552
1553	Sugar beet molasses	750	12.9	16	47	0	0	884	69	16.7	0.77	81	0.34	0.00	0.00	0.90	1553
1554	Sugar cane molasses	750	12.7	14	41	0	0	872	87	16.4	0.78	80	0.35	0.00	0.00	0.90	1554
1555	Tapioca flour	900	15.0	13	20	6	29	922	23	17.6	0.86	95	0.67	0.20	0.76	0.99	1555
1556	Wheat feeds, middlings	880	11.9	129	176	41	86	650	47	18.8	0.63	72	0.73	0.87	0.23	0.82	1556
1557	Wheat feeds, bran	880	10.1	126	170	45	114	603	67	18.6	0.55	61	0.74	0.69	0.22	0.71	1557
1558	Yeast, dried	900	11.7	381	443	11	2	441	102	18.3	0.64	75	0.86	0.40	0.00	0.82	1558
1559	Yeast, wood sugar (dried)	900	12.6	471	523	14	0	381	81	19.2	0.66	81	0.90	0.23	0.00	0.88	1559